The Leach Legacy

The St Ives Pottery and its influence

Marion Whybrow

Sansom & Company

an imprint of Redcliffe Press Ltd., Bristol.

First published in 1996 by Sansom & Company,
an imprint of Redcliffe Press Ltd,
22 Canynge Square, Bristol BS8 3LA
Tel: 0117 973 7207

For my husband Terry
and daughters
Kim and Tracey

ISBN 1 900178 40 0

British Library Cataloguing in Publication Data
A catalogue record for this book is available from
The British Library

Designed and typeset by Steve Leary, Bristol
and printed by The Longdunn Press, Bristol

C O N T E N T S

INTRODUCTION

Bernard Leach, a towering figure in the world of ceramics, was more than a craftsman potter. He was a leader: a teacher of aesthetics and excellence, from whom generations of potters took their inspiration and example. This book pays tribute to Leach's dynamic influence and provides testimony, not only in words, but in portraying the many excellent craftsmen and women who have set up their own potteries and become masters of their craft. In doing this they pay tribute to their working time at the Leach Pottery and their contact with Bernard Leach and his philosophy.

Marion Whybrow   September 1996

FOREWORD

I first bought work by Bernard Leach in 1956 when, on visiting the original Crafts Centre at Hay Hill, I had the good fortune to see being unpacked a vigorous, largely unglazed coffee set of his, to which I immediately laid claim. Later during the same day I met Lucie Rie and Hans Coper for the first time, and my BL purchase at once forged a bond of sympathy, as Lucie had elsewhere seen and greatly admired the same group of pots. Earlier that year I'd written to the Leach Pottery asking where their pots could be seen in the north of England, and been told nowhere as yet on a regular basis. However, the reply had referred me to the Crafts Centre, where on an initial visit I had seen no work by BL but had been able to buy pots by Katharine Pleydell-Bouverie and David Leach.

Before long I had met Bernard Leach himself at Primavera (and was to meet him repeatedly at exhibitions, other pottery occasions and at St Ives), and from then onwards was often in pursuit of other work also of Leach origins or connections, notably pots by Michael Cardew, Michael Leach, Janet Leach, William Marshall, Kenneth Quick, Richard Batterham and Trevor Corser, and by potters influenced from a greater distance, including Henry Hammond, Geoffrey Whiting and Jim Malone, all but one of whom among others I sooner or later met. I also bought more of BL's own pots (including a tenmoku jar with shoulder lugs and with a fish engraved right round it, a choice on which Hans Coper offered congratulations), whilst in 1961 I successfully commissioned from BL a tall jug, sprigged, and with a green ash-clay glaze. Some of these were borrowed back for retrospective exhibitions from 1961 until the late 1970s, or went to Japan in 1980 for the memorial exhibition at Osaka.

Bernard Leach's personality and what he had to say were, like his pots, evocative of strong responses. I continue to feel that his later detractors often seemed to be meanly aiming their invective rather at the work of minor mere imitators (and referred to that as the end product of 'the Leach tradition') than at the man himself and the many remarkable potters whose achievement was assisted by impulses from him which led them either to make their own examinations and interpretations of the particular traditional standards which he personally called upon, or to send down their own roots in his manner into soil of their own choosing. The verdict of potters in general on his life and work was better signalised by the unprecedented assembly in London in his honour when he was ninety.

W A Ismay

THE POTTERY

*'We want from the artist potter the same sort of quality which
we expect from a good author, poet, painter or composer.
Your main objective should be aesthetic, to know good pot from bad pot
and to be able to find your way with your own clear convictions
amidst all the good and bad pots past and present to making
good sincere and honest pots of your own.'*

This is part of a letter from Bernard Leach to his grandson, John, in 1960, in preparing him to meet the commitment and strict requirements that Leach demanded of anyone who came to work at St Ives Pottery, whether clay mixer, apprentice, student, or experienced potter.

After Bernard Leach and Shoji Hamada set up the pottery in St Ives, Cornwall, students began clamouring to work there. Applicants were interviewed and a short trial period arranged when they were carefully judged for their suitability and persistence in learning to develop skills through the necessary work routine of making standard ware. The experience of learning to throw a pot to a determined shape, size and weight, was essential before the development of individual expression. This Leach encouraged through his careful analysis of their pots and in the student acquiring techniques and a critical eye for the aesthetics of form, shape and balance.

Leach felt there was an essential quality that came from throwing and repeating a shape and learning to handle clay. The pots he admired were Korean and Chinese, made by simple craftsmen. He firmly believed that a rhythm developed within the potter through the repeat process which gave life to a pot.'I used to be able to tell which person made the pots in my pottery – the standard ware of cups and bowls and plates. There were eight or ten people working and sometimes I would go around and see some of their work on a shelf and I would say to myself the character of the person who made that is coming through. That is what I want to see. It is a very important thing.'[1]

The central core in Bernard's belief was 'the pot is the man.'

In his final book, *Beyond East and West*, Leach wrote, 'Gradually from all over the world we must have had nearly a hundred students, but there was never any attempt to start anything like classes, as done in schools and American universities. Periodically I talked to them as they learnt their alphabets of clay –

its qualities – its innate demands on a potter – its form and decoration – kiln, slips, glazes, encouraging them to stand on their own feet, both technically and aesthetically, insisting on right standards, but avoiding rules.'[2]

Warren MacKenzie and his wife Alix were the first Americans to become pupils at the Leach Pottery after the war. Warren, on teaching pottery in art school in America said, 'When I taught second year students, who thought they were pretty good and could throw, to show them their weaknesses I produced one of the Leach standard shapes. Make one correctly this term was the assignment. No one ever could.'[3] This underlined Bernard's firm conviction that the workshop was the proper place for learning craft skills.

THE BEGINNING

The St Ives Pottery reaches back to 1920, when Leach, having spent eleven years in China and Japan, left the East to set up a pottery in England with his friend Shoji Hamada, the Japanese potter. It says much for the friendship of the two men that they travelled across the world together to an uncertain future. Certainly for a Japanese man to leave his country was unusual in 1920, and so began a fusion of the art and traditions of East and West, a successful marriage of two different cultures.

At that time, The St Ives Handicraft Guild wished to include a potter and its founder, Mrs Frances Horne, put up £2,500 which Leach matched with a similar sum over a period of time, enabling him to buy the property. The chosen site for the building was three quarters of a mile up hill from St Ives in Cornwall, where a large artists' colony had flourished since the 1880s and was (and still is) one of the foremost colonies in Britain. At the turn of the century 30 artists from St Ives had their work hung in the Royal Academy.

The arrival of the artists, who rented net lofts for studios, preserved the old cottages in the fishing quarter, and provided employment, helped ensure the town's economic survival. The Stennack stream, by which the pottery was built, carried the sediment of old tin mines down to the sea and small town harbour, once famous for its fishing industry. Both tin mining and fishing were now in decline. Leach and Hamada identified with the arts and crafts movement of William Morris and the making of functional ware for the ordinary household, but in practice they began producing individual studio pots, designed largely for exhibition in galleries, rather than creating a country workshop of domestic ware to sell from the premises. They built a Japanese, wood-fired, three-chambered climbing kiln on a slope, the first of its kind in Britain, enabling the potter to fire one chamber after another with varying temperatures. Each chamber measured 180 centimetres height and width, by 120 centimetres front to back.

St Ives was not the most promising place in which to set up a pottery in the 1920s. Apart from its then remoteness, Cornwall had long been denuded of its trees and finding fuel for the kiln was one of their first difficulties, as well as the search for local clays and natural materials for glazes. Together they tramped the countryside in their quest for these vital elements.

The building of the pottery aroused the curiosity of local people. It had been reported that an industrial plant was being established which would solve the unemployment problems of the town. Leach wrote to the *St Ives Times,* explaining the position:

> Sir: As there seem to be various rumours in the town that the pottery which we are now building below Penbeagle Farm is to be a large industrial concern, employing local labour, I shall be glad of the opportunity of briefly stating the facts in order to prevent any sense of disappointment which might otherwise arise.
>
> The works are to be of a private nature and on quite a small scale. For the first year or two, at least, we shall not employ more than the occasional odd labour of one or two men. How the work will develop later on remains to be seen. Our object is to turn out genuine handicrafts of quality rather than machine craft in quantity.
>
> The former is difficult to find now in England, as it has been driven out by modern industry and applied science. In the Cornish pitcher, made at the Lake Pottery at Truro, it is still possible to see something of the spirit of the old English pottery, but the ware is a very simple one and unsuited to many modern purposes.
>
> I have long been studying pottery in the Far East, where the traditions of old craftsmanship and beauty have not yet been driven out, and the various kinds of earthenware, stoneware and porcelain, which my Japanese friend and assistant, Mr Hamada and I will make, will be an attempt to combine the fine old craft of both East and West to our present needs. With many thanks for the courtesy of your page.
>
> Yours truly, Bernard Leach.[4]

After the completion of the building, which Leach and Hamada had designed themselves, one of the workmen, George Dunn, an ex-miner and fisherman, offered his services as general labourer for the pottery. This help was welcomed by the two potters, who were building the interior, constructing the kiln, digging for clay and searching for wood. George soon found himself sawing 200 tons of wood for the kiln, bought from the Great Western Railway, and helping to make benches, shelving and other equipment. He remained a loyal worker for many years. His son Horatio took over in 1937 until his retirement in 1958. Horatio died in 1994.

Bernard bought the 14-roomed Count House in Carbis Bay for his wife, three girls and two boys, David and Michael, who both became potters. Grandson John also became a potter. The house was once owned by the captain of Wheal Providence tin mine. It had also been the home of psychologist Dr Havelock Ellis, president of the World League for Sexual Reform, and his wife Edith, who raised prize bulls on the small portion of land round the house, and wrote novels in the vernacular about the local St Ives population.

THE WORKING PARTNERSHIP

Shoji made his home at the pottery. Leach and Hamada enjoyed working together, talking over meals round the open fireplace, sharing the same ideals and values, learning from each other and their experience of making pots and so fusing their ideas of the meeting of two cultures. They were producing English slipware and Oriental stoneware and hard porcelain. Leach considered that he, Hamada and Cardew revived the technique of seventeenth-century English slipware, which was rediscovered accidentally when Leach and Hamada sliced through a sandwich of blackberry jam and cream and saw how the substances fused.

But the beginning was essentially an experimental period when they made mistakes, with many of their firings ending up smashed in the Stennack stream. But they were pioneers and felt they were establishing the era of the artist-craftsman potter, the educated artist taking up a job which was previously relegated to the village workshop. The thinking man would replace the artisan's hand-made craft which had been washed away by the Industrial Revolution, when all pots were made to perfection and in thousands, and reinstate the idea of truth to materials and an appreciation of the beauty of simple design, quiet colours and the personal touch. They both admired Korean and Chinese ceramics, as well as medieval English pots and early Japanese tea ware.

The high cost of kiln losses meant the pots were fairly expensive but both Leach and Hamada managed to exhibit locally, on Show Day, when artists opened their studios to the general public, and in the Cotswold and Patterson's

Bernard Leach and Shoji Hamada loading the St Ives kiln, 1920s.

Three-chambered Japanese climbing kiln and (left) Leach kick-wheel.

Leach Pottery cottage, and The Count House, the Leach family home.

Coleshill, 1929: Bernard Leach with Soetsu Yanagi, Shoji Hamada, Henry Bergen, Katharine Pleydell-Bouverie, Michael Cardew, Katharine's mother and Norah Braden.

Galleries in Bond Street, London. They also sold their pots to Japan. Their Japanese friends were sending generous amounts of money to Cornwall from sales to help finance the pottery. Sales in Britain, however, were poor. The pots were considered faulty because of the impurities in the natural clays, textures, and the variations in the glazes, compared with the smooth perfection achieved by industrial methods of production. An American collector, Henry Bergen, acquired much of their early experimental work. As well as introducing them to other collectors, he came to St Ives and joined enthusiastically in kiln firings, as did other friends who were prepared to help round the clock at a time when firings could take up to 36 hours.

RAKU

Leach began his study of raku in Tokyo and, after being established a few years, used the technique to help advertise the pottery in St Ives. The public were invited to attend afternoon demonstrations of low temperature Japanese raku-fired pots in a small purpose-built kiln. They decorated their biscuit purchases and watched as they were glazed and fired and afterwards carried them home. It didn't actually achieve much in extra sales. Bernard had intended to extend hospitality: 'teas of a good home-made character will be provided in the pottery cottage now being built. The furnishing of the new room will be by some of the best English craftsmen and women.'[5] The teas were provided and good Cornish fare served by Muriel, Bernard's first wife, but the proposed furnishing of the room did not materialise.

Leach did in fact design furniture. The first had been a chair made in Japan to support his long legs. Over six feet in height, he had grown tired of sitting on the floor, Japanese-style. For the pottery, he designed a modified version of the kick wheel which was made in wood by Robin Nance, a local furniture maker, and which is still in use at the pottery. It seems to have been manufactured commercially at some time and advertised as the 'modified Leach Pottery wheel'.

After little more than three years the Japanese climbing kiln was in a state of collapse because of their inexperience and the varieties of wood used which caused choking in the firing and problems with the glazes. Fortunately Tsuronosuke Matsubayashi, an engineer and kiln specialist, and the product of 39 generations of family potters in Kyoto, arrived from Japan. He rebuilt and redesigned the three-chambered climbing kiln to a more efficient standard. During his stay in St Ives he exhibited with the local print society 'a study of Japanese medlars'. He remained at the pottery until 1924. Hamada returned to Japan in 1923, after an earthquake had devastated the city of Tokyo and he was unable to contact his family. Hamada married in Japan and built his own kiln in Mashiko in 1930, where four boys and two girls were born. Two of the boys, Shinsaku and Atsuya, became potters and one grandson, Tomoo.

In Mashiko, Hamada adopted the lifestyle of a Zen monk and the belief that where he lived and worked was the place he achieved a higher dimension. His pots were linked to daily life and usefulness. Hamada liked to call himself, simply, 'a potter'. One tradition that Hamada took back to Mashiko was the Cornish pasty, a shell-shaped pastry case filled with chopped beef and vegetables. According to Tomoo, his grandson, it is still made and appreciated in Mashiko today.

The first student and others

The pottery in St Ives almost accidentally acquired its first student when Michael Cardew, who had decided he wanted to work with Leach, turned up on his doorstep at the Count House in 1923 with Shoji Hamada, who had accompanied him there from the pottery. Cardew was not totally without experience of potting but on meeting Bernard soon realised that 'what I naturally liked was not necessarily the last word, and that many kinds of pot which were at first inaccessible to me had qualities which I would be able to learn about if I tried.' [6]

Cardew felt he wasn't entirely acceptable to Leach on their first acquaintance. Fortunately they shared an enthusiasm for English slipware and so in July 1923, after finishing his studies at Oxford, he joined the staff. He was at first disheartened by his inability to throw an order for two dozen mugs to a uniform size and shape and learnt that 'unless you can do this you are only an improviser, not a thrower.'[7] After three years Michael established his own pottery at Winchcombe in Gloucestershire. In 1939, from a dilapidated property, he built the Wenford Bridge Pottery at Bodmin in Cornwall, which remains in the family and is worked by his son Seth and grandson Ara.

Students continued to arrive. They came for a matter of weeks or a year or two. Several skilled potters arrived with the primary aim of having access to Bernard and the experience of working at the Leach Pottery. Others studied at art school and worked there part time. Henry Hammond spent two weeks with Bernard just after the second world war before teaching at West Surrey College of Art. He had studied pottery under William Staite Murray at the Royal College of Art, London after attending design courses run by Edward Bawden and Eric Ravilious. Helen Pincombe worked for six weeks at the pottery before becoming a student of William Staite Murray. She went on to teach at the RCA and Guildford and Willesden Schools of Art. She ran her own workshop in Oxshott, Surrey from 1949 until she retired in 1972.

Staite Murray himself had visited St Ives in 1923, when Hamada taught him to make footrings to his pots. He was Head of Pottery at the Royal College of Art from 1925 to the outbreak of war. As a practising artist, he saw the future of studio pottery more as fine art than craft, and had no time for the 'ethical pot'.

Another visitor was Lucie Rie, who visited Bernard at Dartington, and also travelled down from London to St Ives, making buttons and beads at the bench. She had turned her hand to this skill when, following the war, attractive buttons for dress-making were in short supply. Mary Gibson-Horrocks remembers: 'I sat next to her handling my jugs and was fascinated with her work.' Lucie Rie's buttons are exhibited in the fashion collection of the Victoria and Albert Museum, London. The delicacy and elegance of her pots is in sharp contrast to those of Leach, but they admired each other's work. Bernard would often stay with Lucie in her Albion Mews studio flat on his trips to London, and

Michael Cardew
decorating slipware:
Winchcombe, 1925.

Charlotte Epton at Leach
Pottery, c. 1928.

David Leach lifting a thrown pot from the wheel head, 1939.

Pottery group, 1947: Bernard, Kenneth Quick, David Leach, Joe Benney, Aileen Newton, Mary Gibson-Horrocks and Horatio Dunn.

she stayed at Bernard's flat in Barnaloft when in St Ives. Artist Willie Barns-Graham remembers her sitting outside her window on Porthmeor beach.

Others included Barbara Millard, William Worrall and John Coney, who potted at Glastonbury, and Kenneth Murray who trained potters in Nigeria. David Leach joined his father at the pottery in 1930 and was taught to throw by Muriel Bell, later to establish a pottery at Malvern. He was also instructed by Harry Davis, from whom David said he learned more throwing skills than anyone else. Paul Barron, who later taught at Farnham College of Art with Henry Hammond, was taught by two Leach potters, Norah Braden and Helen Pincombe. John Bew arrived at the pottery in 1938, and later joined a Quaker school and taught pottery skills to boys from a local mining community in the Rhondda. In 1942 he supplied pottery for the John Lewis store in London from his Odney Pottery at Cookham-on-Thames, Berkshire.

Nirmala Patwardhan, born in Hyderabad, India, in 1928, worked with Bernard in the late 1950s and also with Ray Finch at the Winchcombe Pottery, where she conducted a number of her glaze experiments. In 1984 she published *Handbook for Potters* for potters working in India. Brenda Potter, born Tinklin, worked for 18 months at the Leach Pottery from 1978 to 1980 after a two-year apprenticeship at the Mask Pottery in Penzance and before doing a BA Hons in Fine Art at Ravensbourne College in Kent. She went on to teach ceramics and art and is now head of a comprehensive school in Portsmouth:'but my first love is still ceramics. I have a wheel and kiln at home and still do commissions.'

ARTISTS AND SOCIETIES

Soon after arriving in St Ives Bernard Leach and family, with Hamada, joined the St Ives Arts Club, a professional club for painters, sculptors, musicians, architects and writers. During those early years Bernard and members of the family took as their guests, Matsubayashi, Michael Cardew, Norah Braden, Katharine Pleydell-Bouverie, Ada Mason, William Worrall, Muriel Bell, John Coney, Bernard Forrester, Valerie Bond, Dick Kendall, Patrick Heron, Mary Gibson-Horrocks and Beryl Debney, all of whom worked at the pottery at various times. The Leach family enjoyed a long association with the Arts Club and friends of the children were allowed access to clay and the wheel at the pottery.

In 1926 the St Ives Society of Artists was established from a break-away group of the Arts Club where, Bernard said at a meeting, they should have a gallery to display their work. The first exhibition space was set up in the Porthmeor Studios. In 1949, following an acrimonious split between the modern and traditionalist factions in the Society,* the Penwith Society of Arts

*For an eye-witness account of the fateful meeting in 1949, see Sven Berlin's *The Coat of Many Colours.*

was formed by the modern artists with Ben Nicholson and Barbara Hepworth at their head. Bernard and David Leach were among them, both exhibiting frequently in the Society and serving on the committee in the early 1960s.

Bernard was active in the artists' community in working for the good of the town and its environment. In the early 1960s he was among many famous artist signatories in a letter to *The Times*, protesting at the Admiralty's plans to use the moorland (an area of outstanding natural beauty) for troop landing exercises. Leach, Hepworth and Heron also joined forces to help block planning permission, in which they were successful, for a holiday complex at a former clay works. In 1962 Bernard Leach was awarded the CBE in the New Year's Honours list to mark his fifty years as a potter. He was on a lecture tour in New Zealand when the news came through. CBEs for artistic achievement were also awarded to Barbara Hepworth in 1958 and to Patrick Heron in 1977. In 1968 Leach, Hepworth and Nicholson were granted the Freedom of the Borough of St Ives in recognition of their services to the town and their international contribution to the arts. Exhibitions of pottery, sculpture and painting were held throughout St Ives in celebration.

DARTINGTON

In 1927 Bernard and Muriel Leach drove to Devon to see Dorothy and Leonard Elmhirst, who were establishing a progressive school and a centre for rural arts and crafts in a beautiful but run down medieval estate at Dartington Hall. Dorothy invited Bernard to transfer his pottery there and join the community but, instead, he recommended Sylvia Fox-Strangways, who had worked at St Ives, to run their first pottery classes. Sylvia (known as Jane) retired within a couple of years, in 1929, because of ill health but remained in close association with Dartington throughout her life. Examples of her work can be seen at Dartington Hall, where some of the fire surrounds are decorated with tiles made by her during her three years there.

In 1931/32 Leach did establish a small workshop there, producing traditional slipware, and taught part-time at the Foxhole School at Dartington, while the Elmhirsts built a new pottery at Shinners Bridge, close by the estate. Before its completion Bernard was in Japan and David Leach was the first teacher at the pottery. A year later, in 1934, the Elmhirsts sponsored David for a management and scientific course at Stoke Technical College in the heart of industrial pottery. He undertook this with the intention of improving output and efficiency at the Dartington Pottery. Bernard Forrester, who had been working at St Ives, moved to Dartington to teach while the Leach Pottery was run by

Harry Davis, who carried the main burden of production in the years 1933-37. Bernard Leach described Harry as 'the only fast, well-trained thrower on the potter's wheel who had ever studied with me.'[8] May Scott joined the small team, and eventually married Harry.

From Stoke-on-Trent David did not return to Dartington, but to St Ives. Having acquired knowledge and confidence, he developed some of the techniques learned in industry and applied them to the small pottery. With financial help from Dartington a certain amount of modernisation took place, including a change to oil firing and the introduction of machinery to reduce time in preparing clay. He also gave up slipware in favour of the more adaptable stoneware. Another lesson learned was that if the pottery was to run smoothly a more permanent staff would be needed. They decided to recruit and train local boys straight from school. The first apprentice was William Marshall, who joined the staff in 1938 and became a skilled thrower, foreman and mainstay of the Leach Pottery for about 40 years.

BERNARD LEACH IN JAPAN

In Japan a craft movement, named Mingei (art of the people), was forming and Leach was invited to visit by the leader, his close friend Soetsu Yanagi. In 1934 Dorothy Elmhirst generously financed the trip and provided the money for Mark Tobey, an American painter, to go as travelling companion. He and Bernard had become friends when they were teaching at Dartington. It was Tobey who introduced Leach to the Baha'i faith, which, attracted by their belief in the universal brotherhood of man, Bernard then followed to the end of his days.

While in Japan Leach took the opportunity of visiting potteries in remote areas, learning to improvise with the materials to hand. At Mashiko he was hosted by Hamada's family. The friends renewed their pleasure in potting together and firing the kilns. Years later, in 1957, Hamada's son Atsuya came to work in St Ives and his second son, Shinsaku, visited with Hamada in 1963. Hamada returned to Britain several times and in 1966 he brought his wife Kazue and daughter. The cosmopolitan team working at the Leach Pottery at that time – from Canada, Australia, Scandinavia and America – were honoured to meet him.

At Kyoto Leach explored the workshops of Kanjiro Kawai, who had an eight-chambered kiln. Here Leach made porcelain pots. In Tokyo he resumed a working relationship with Kenkichi Tomimoto with whom he shared the title of Seventh Kenzan inherited from their Japanese pottery master Ogata Kenzan in

Bernard Leach with Shoji Hamada in Japan, 1934; they opened a joint kiln at Mashiko.

1912. At Matsue, on Lake Shinji, he met the potter Michitada Funaki, whose son Kenji would come to England for a year in 1967 to work with David Leach at Lowerdown Pottery in Devon, and again in 1977 to visit Bernard at St Ives.

At Abiko Leach renewed his friendship with the Yanagi family on whose land he had built a kiln and workroom in 1917. He learnt of the construction of a folk craft museum being planned by Yanagi, Kawai and Hamada in Tokyo. Their idea was to find and exhibit domestic hand-made crafts in cloth, metalwork, lacquer, furniture, prints, pots, and every available artefact made by the 'unknown craftsman'. Their intention was to raise the level of these traditional crafts, which were under threat from Japan's desperate bid to launch itself into the modern world. Leach played a major role and travelled hundreds of miles with them, choosing and collecting samples of country crafts for exhibition in Tokyo and Osaka. In 1929 Yanagi had founded the Japanese Craft Movement, the same year as he and Hamada visited England. Yanagi's dream of establishing a Japanese Folkcraft Museum in Tokyo was realised in 1936.

A POTTER'S BOOK

Leach's experiences in Japan led him to write *A Potter's Book*, and Dorothy Elmhirst, as well as sponsoring his trip to Japan, provided the means for his research and working time to write the book. It was published in 1940 and ever since has been invaluable to anyone determined to follow the craft. It has been translated into many languages and, with sales exceeding 130,000, has never been out of print. As well as a practical text book it has proved an inspiration to aspiring potters. 'I felt there was a gap. I saw the need for interpretation, and with the hope of assisting young English potters, began to write *A Potter's Book*. Fortunately I had always kept diaries and notes covering standards, methods and ideals. I had no idea of the wide response the book would receive.'[9]

Too many to name have been converted to ceramics through reading the book, which soon acquired the soubriquet of 'the Potter's Bible'. Michael Casson was one who succumbed to its influence. He later taught pottery at Harrow School of Art. Eileen Lewenstein, in her final year of teacher training at London University, read the book, gained experience as a potter, set up a studio in Hampstead and taught pottery at Hornsey College of Art. Ray Finch, who took over the Winchcombe Pottery from Michael Cardew, acknowledged the book's importance in his formative years.

The Irish potter, Peter Brennan wrote to Bernard through the publisher and on visiting the Leach Pottery was invited by David and Bernard to become an apprentice. He turned down the offer, having established a pottery studio with

Victor Waddington. Molly Attrill, potter from the Isle of Wight, says that she was 'steeped in the Leach St Ives ethos', through reading the book, which prompted her to go on a Leach pilgrimage. Michael Leach taught her to pot. She then studied at West Surrey College of Art and Design, Farnham, under Henry Hammond. There she met Marsha Cox, a former Leach student, and helped her set up her pottery in Ontario, Canada.

Although Leach guided students in aesthetics, standards, the use of basic materials and a genuine love for the craft in his teaching and writing, he did not want to produce copyists. In a letter to Warren MacKenzie in 1968 Bernard wrote, 'I don't expect Lucie Rie or Michael Cardew or Hans Coper or Hamada to like, or do, just what I like or do.' Three of the potters he most admired owed nothing to his style and technique. Janet Leach was an American whose pots he described as strong, free and adventurous. Lucie Rie came from Vienna and her work was quiet and refined, reflecting her personality. Hans Coper from Germany showed positive and modern traits with references to older roots. He felt their backgrounds allowed them a certain cultural freedom. However, a Leach tradition did grow from his teachings and he attracted many admirers and followers. For himself, Leach said he enjoyed making a pulled handle and was probably more proficient in this technique than in throwing.

THE WAR YEARS

During the war years David Leach and Bill Marshall were serving in the forces while Bernard joined the Home Guard along with the artists Adrian Stokes, Leonard Fuller, Denis Mitchell and Borlase Smart. Leach, by now divorced from Muriel, married his second wife, Laurie Cookes, who was secretary at the pottery. They, too, eventually separated and divorced. Two conscientious objectors who were detailed to work at the pottery were Dick Kendall – who later taught at Camberwell School of Art and married Bernard's daughter, Jessamine – and Patrick Heron, art critic and painter. Heron had lived in St Ives as a child and in the 1950s he and his wife Delia bought Eagle's Nest, a house on a promontory on the road to Zennor, formerly the home of the landscape painter, Will Arnold-Forster. Heron was commissioned to design a stained glass window for the opening of the Tate Gallery, St Ives in 1993. His large areas of colour were achieved by the process of laminating layers of coloured glass on to strengthened glass, rather than breaking up the design with the usual leaded strips. It is the largest window of its kind in the world.

Heron spent 14 months at the pottery and said of Bernard that 'he has demonstrated the aesthetic parallel existing between Sung and medieval

English pottery – thus creating a genuine East-West synthesis; and, in doing this, he has given us a ceramic idiom very much in accord with aspects of modern art. One can compare him to Henry Moore in some ways: both by-passed the Renaissance.'[10]

In 1941 Edward Bouverie-Hoyton, principal of Penzance School of Art, set up a pottery department and Bernard Leach was the first potter to teach there. Sons David and Michael Leach were also later to teach at Penzance.

The Leach Pottery was out of action for a time during the war when a stray bomb partly demolished the cottage and workshop. Ironically, there was an increased demand for pots and, after repairs, production in standard ware was going at full tilt. Bernard made the prototypes and drew them on cards with dimensions for whoever was making the cups, saucers, bowls, jugs, and other domestic items.

Four women worked at the pottery in the war years: Aileen Newton (died c.1983), Valerie Bond, Mary Gibson-Horrocks and namesake Margaret Leach. Mary, Valerie and Bernard lived in the pottery cottage, and Margaret in a cottage opposite, but all shared in the household chores. A list of duties was drawn up each week by Bernard whose self-imposed task was to do the laundry. After the war they were joined from Ireland by Grattan Freyer and his French wife Madeleine.

In 1942, Alfred Wallis, the primitive St Ives painter died. Bernard Leach joined Adrian Stokes and Margaret Mellis, Ben Nicholson, Miriam and Naum Gabo and the writer George Manning-Sanders among those attending the funeral. Later, Leach made a ceramic tiled plaque for the grave in Barnoon Cemetery, showing a figure entering a lighthouse. It reads, 'Alfred Wallis Artist and Mariner'. Wallis turned painter at the age of 70 as a refuge from loneliness after the death of his wife. His untutored style was much admired by the modern painters, especially Ben Nicholson and Christopher Wood who had discovered Wallis on an excursion to St Ives in 1928. Jim Ede, then assistant curator at the Tate Gallery, London, bought for himself many of Wallis's paintings which can now be seen, along with Leach pots and work by other St Ives artists, at Kettle's Yard, Cambridge.

BERNARD AND DAVID FORM A PARTNERSHIP

David returned from war service and went into partnership with his father in 1946. They were joined by Michael Leach in 1950 and there followed a period of stability to 1955. Demand for Leach standard ware in the post-war years grew to such an extent that London stores like Heals, Liberty and John Lewis wanted everything they could produce. David was now largely responsible for the organisation and running of the pottery, but the guiding hand was Bernard's, and pots were still made to his design and purpose. David said, 'He was always the artist, creator and inspiration. I was the right-hand man. Bernard would make the first pot and I would make the first interpretation. I taught the team of people.'[11] When David and Michael left in 1955 to set up their own separate potteries in Devon, Bill Marshall became foreman in charge of the team.

A catalogue from the time shows over 100 items from egg cups to casseroles, along with individual pots, 'the personal work of Bernard or David Leach or other members of the Pottery, whose seal they usually bear'.[12] Staffing levels were increased and joining as an apprentice in 1945 was Kenneth Quick, a local lad, and Joe Benney, who became the glazer and glaze maker.

The first post-war exhibition of individual pots was held at the Berkeley Gallery in London in 1946. The invitation card was designed by the printer, Guido Morris, with the words running down the paper to replicate Japanese writing. Morris was working in St Ives at the time and designed many artists' catalogues and exhibition posters, including the famous 'Catalo' for the Crypt Group of painters set up by Sven Berlin, Peter Lanyon and John Wells. A photograph taken outside the Berkeley Gallery shows artists, friends, exhibitors, relatives and students. Afterwards they lunched at a Chinese restaurant in Soho, before going on to the BBC for the showing of a film taken at the St Ives Pottery. Mary Gibson-Horrocks remembers that about 30 people attended and afterwards they all went back to Lucie Rie's flat for tea and her famous sponge cake.

Valerie Bond, working at the pottery during 1946 described Bernard Leach as 'the father to all the artists. Many of the young and struggling artists, now in the Tate, used to visit the pottery. It was the home they loved to come to. They were all glad to talk to Bernard.'[13] They went there at tea time and in the evenings. The visitors included the painters Ben Nicholson and Adrian Stokes, the printer Guido Morris, other potters working in the town, and the sculptors Barbara Hepworth, Sven Berlin and Naum Gabo. 'One memorable day Gabo spoke to some of us for two hours in his studio about his work and the Constructivist movement.'[14] Valerie recalls the first time she met Gabo. 'Bernard said he was taking us to see a friend. We walked across the fields and the door of the bungalow was opened by an excited little man. He just said, "come and see" and led us through to a room, which was unlit except for the moon shining through a construction he had just made. We all stood there in silence and amazement. It was so beautiful.'[15]

Bernard in discussion with
Mary Gibson-Horrocks, Valerie
Bond and David Leach, 1946.

Firing the St Ives kiln.

THE LEACH POTTERY

THE PRESENT MEMBERS OF THE LEACH POTTERY, BERNARD LEACH,
DAVID LEACH, HORATIO DUNN, FRANK VIBERT, AILEEN NEWTON,
VALERIE BOND, MARY GIBSON HORROCKS AND KENNETH QUICK,
INVITE YOU TO A PRIVATE VIEW AT THE CLOSE OF THE TWENTY-
SIXTH ANNIVERSARY EXHIBITION AT THE BERKELEY GALLERIES,
20, DAVIES STREET, W.1, ON THE AFTERNOON OF SATURDAY, JUNE
29TH. 1946, TO BE FOLLOWED BY A CHINESE DINNER. R.S.V.P.

THE PRINTER

GUIDO MORRIS

Guido Morris-printed invitation, 1946.

Outside the Berkeley Gallery, London, 1946: from left – Lucie Rie, Sam Haile, William Ohly of Berkeley Gallery, Laurie Cookes, Jean Smith, –, Patrick Heron, Bunty Smith, Kenneth Quick, Dorothy Kemp, Aileen Newton, Delia Heron, Jessamine Leach, Jane Fox-Strangways, Harry Davis, Bernard Leach, – .Sitting, front – Dicon Nance, Dick Kendall, Frank Vibert, Margaret Leach, Mariel Cardew, Valerie Bond, Horatio Dunn, Michael Leach. David Leach took the photograph.

Leach Pottery, 1948: Joe Benney, Michael Leach, Frank Vibert, Margaret Leach, –, Horatio Dunn, Bill Marshall, Kenneth Quick, Cecil Baugh and Anne Marie Backer-Mohr.

Leach stoneware plate, attributed to B.L. and preserve pot listed in 1959-60 catalogue as 'B.L. decorated'.

Leach Pottery tea set, 1936.

Bernard Leach tiles on gravestone of Edgar Skinner, pottery business manager in 1922: Barnoon Cemetery, St Ives.

Horse and rider earthenware in mottled orange and yellow colouring, intended for roof ridge.

Bernard Leach's tribute to Alfred Wallis, 1942: gravestone, Barnoon Cemetery, St Ives.

David Leach at the pottery, with Horatio Dunn, 1950.

Peter Wood handling soup bowls, 1954.

Cecil Baugh and Horatio Dunn, 1949.

Bernard Leach decorating a bowl.

Derek Emms making coffee jugs at the Leach Pottery, 1954.

THE LEACH POTTERY

Catalogue

1954

Bernard & David Leach

1954 catalogue and, below, decoration from an earlier catalogue.

Domestic ware offered in the 1954 catalogue.

Wilhelmina Barns-Graham, a painter friend of Bernard's for 37 years, remembers him as a true friend to all who knew him: 'So many people turned to him with their troubles. He listened to you as though you were the most important person in the world. People looked upon Bernard as a guru.' She first met him when he came to her studio in St Ives and admired her work.

During the Festival of Britain in 1951 an exhibition – '15 Artists and Craftsmen from around St Ives' – was organised by Denis Mitchell at the Mansard Gallery at Heals of Tottenham Court Road, London. The catalogue was printed by Guido Morris and the exhibitors were painters Ben Nicholson, Peter Lanyon, Patrick Heron, John Wells, Misome Peile, Bryan Wynter, Alfred Wallis, Terry Frost, Tom Early, Willie Barns-Graham, sculptors Barbara Hepworth, Sven Berlin and Denis Mitchell, the potter Bernard Leach and printer Guido Morris. It was Leach who had first introduced Mitchell to Barbara Hepworth as someone who could handle material. Denis worked in her studio for ten years before buying a house and studio in Newlyn and becoming a sculptor in his own right.

DARTINGTON INTERNATIONAL CONFERENCE 1952

In 1952 Bernard Leach met up with his friends Hamada and Yanagi, representing Japan, at the Dartington Conference in Devon, an international gathering of potters and weavers to consider the role of the craftsman in the post-war period. It was the first of its kind and Lucie Rie, Hans Coper, Michael Cardew, Katharine Pleydell-Bouverie, Warren MacKenzie, Muriel Rose and many others associated with Leach attended. An exhibition featuring British craftsmen from 1920 to 1952 was organised and toured nationally.

Over one hundred delegates arrived from Europe, America, Asia and Africa to demonstrate and display their crafts, to lecture, and discuss their philosophies. One such lecture was given by Patrick Heron – 'Submerged Rhythm – A Potter's Aesthetic' – in which he summed up the significance of the work of Bernard Leach and the similarity of the potter and painter in the creative act.

At the end of the conference Leach, Hamada and Yanagi, at the invitation of the Society of Contemporary Arts in Washington, travelled across America, lecturing, demonstrating, exhibiting their work, talking about ceramics and the various aspects of arts and crafts recently raised at Dartington. The following year they toured Japan with a similar agenda. Willie Barns-Graham recalls: 'When Bernard was in Japan he sent letters on long yellow sheets of paper with drawings which we had to pass to a wide circle of friends.' Leach kept copious notes of his travels in Japan and in 1960 recorded his experiences in *A Potter in Japan 1952-55*.

It was at Black Mountain College in America that sculptor and potter, Janet Darnell met Leach and Hamada. The meeting changed her life. She was captured by Hamada's approach to potting and his easy flowing movements in throwing on the wheel. As her friendship with Bernard grew she asked him to recommend her as a student to Hamada. Hamada agreed. It was a major departure, as in Japan at that time women were allowed to help in stacking the kilns and routine manual jobs, but not in actual pot making.

Janet arrived in Japan in the spring of 1954 to a letter from Soetsu Yanagi giving her directions:

Dear Miss Janet Darnell,

I think Leach has told you that your going to Mashiko will be on Wednesday morning (9 inst) Please come to Takumi craft shop at 9 o'clock in the morning. Your luggages which are now in our Museum will be sent to Takumi by that time. The train will leave Ueno station at 10am. Hamada or his son will meet you at the Utsunomiya station.

In haste, Yours truly, Soetsu Yanagi

At Mashiko she found Hamada's family glazing and stacking his eight-chambered climbing kiln with Hamada surrounded by pots issuing instructions and decorating in rhythmic movements. She and Bernard were overawed by his deft handling of hundreds of pots which flowed through his hands. When Bernard asked how he did it he replied, 'I simply look at the pot and ask what it wants.'[16] His way of working was totally intuitive.

On the advice of Hamada, and after six months travelling with him and Bernard to traditional pottery villages, Janet chose to work in the remote mountain village of Tamba, where pottery has been made for over one thousand years. She had not reckoned that she was of great news value. 'I had the mistaken idea that I was going to an isolated area where I could work quietly in the prescribed study method of the East.'[17] Instead, she found herself the first foreigner to work there and the only woman in Japan using the potter's wheel. Janet lived with the Ichino family, living a simple life, but enjoying the warmth and kindness extended to her, making pots and firing in the cave-like kilns. While she was working in Tamba, she would travel to Mashiko for Hamada's glazing and kiln firings and to listen to his advice.

Bernard Leach making pots in Hamada's workshop, 1953.

Janet in Japan: with Tomimoto at Kyoto,1955, and in kimono.

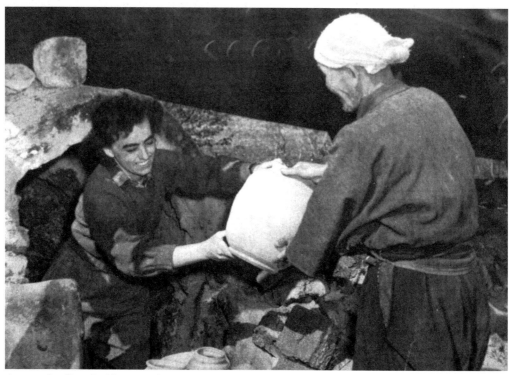

Janet unloading the kiln at Tamba, Japan in 1954; and, below, Shoji Hamada at Mashiko, 1954 from Janet's album.

Janet in Japan, 1955; Shoji Hamada in 1954/55, and Yanagi, Bernard Leach and Hamada at Dartington, 1952.

In 1956, after two years of intense study in Japan, where she felt she had fully realised herself as a potter, Janet came to England to marry Bernard. They set up house in the pottery cottage and Janet was immediately engaged in running the showroom, seeing visitors, organising the work load, as well as continuing to produce her own individual pieces. She believed in the standard ware but declined to make it. Bernard was heavily committed to making pots for international exhibitions.

Janet and Bernard dispensed with the apprenticeship system and engaged more advanced young potters from the art schools for a two-year period. 'We had four Americans, five Canadians, three New Zealanders, four Australians, three Indians, two French, one Belgian, a Dane and a goodly number of English.'[18] Bernard would select the students with a short trial period to judge their quality and potential. Janet bought a small house near the Barbara Hepworth Museum for the students so they could live their own lives and be free of restrictions.

The young potters were encouraged to produce individual pots, as well as developing their skills in the necessarily repetitive standard ware which paid their wages. It was a strict workshop discipline, but once acquired, was the foundation for their own success as potters. Janet and Bernard urged them to keep in mind that although the potter is making a hundred mugs, one person buys and uses one mug, and it must be the best that the potter can produce.

In the Leach Potttery standard ware catalogue for 1970 Bernard wrote:'I have been challenged as to why, after the Leach Pottery has been in existence for half a century, we still think that there is validity in producing and training the student-potters to make our standard catalogued ware. I firmly believe that no one can really teach anyone anything, but students may teach themselves by our words, example, good materials, throwing and firing techniques. Even today a standard of beauty and fine workmanship can emerge from a group, but the desire, the goodwill and the latency must be there.'

As demands on Bernard for his pots, for travels abroad, for lecturing, and for his writing increased, Bill Marshall gradually took over the supervision of standard ware and helped Bernard by throwing some of his larger pots. The climbing kiln, which needed at least four experienced potters to fire it, was gradually abandoned and replaced with a smaller oil-fired kiln. A separate kiln was built for the firing of experimental pots and the workshops were kept open in the evenings and weekends so that students could develop individual expression alongside their technical skills. After a successful firing Janet would

Bill Marshall and Eleanor de Silva, c.1957.

Shoji Hamada's visit to St Ives in 1963: the group includes Ian Steel, Warren MacKenzie, Mick Henry, Shinsaku, Bernard, Hamada, Janet, John Reeve, Glen Lewis, Mirek Smisek, Jack Worseldine.

St Ives in 1963: Hamada with son Shinsaku.

... and Bernard Leach with Mirek Smisek.

From one master to another: Hamada and Leach, Mashiko in 1967.

Bernard Leach watches Shoji Hamada working on the potter's wheel.

provide a celebratory feast in the pottery. Bernard would discuss each piece with a highly critical eye and spared no one. He was a hard task master, but one who also gave encouragement. High standard items were priced by Bernard and sold through the showroom or other suitable venues.

BERNARD LEACH RETIRES FROM POTTING

With Janet to manage the pottery, Bernard was now free to write books, visit Japan, concentrate on exhibiting and to receive many honours bestowed on him by this country and Japan. In 1974, with his eyesight failing, he gave up potting and eventually moved to a flat overlooking Porthmeor beach in St Ives, where he continued his writing by dictating into a tape recorder. He entertained artists and writers and many visitors, and continued to advise the students who came to the Leach Pottery to work by inviting them to tea at the flat at Number 4 Barnaloft. His window overlooked the wild Atlantic ocean where surfers rode mountainous waves and high tide lapped the walls of the building. To his right was the Island with the little chapel of St Nicholas on its summit, decorated with a few Leach floor tiles. To the left Clodgy Point and Mans Head, outcrops of rocks which led to the wild moorland countryside known as West Penwith, and to the village of Zennor, six miles away. Bernard's

Father and son: Bernard with David Leach on a visit to Dartington in the 1970s.

After-the-firing feast: Janet Leach centre left, with Sylvia
Hardaker on her left. 1968.

Hamada and Cecil Baugh at Mashiko, 1973.

Mr and Mrs Hamada and daughter meet old and new friends at the Leach Pottery in 1966.

Janet Leach at the pottery in 1975.

poor vision did not diminish his appreciation of his immediate surroundings.

'When (semi) blindness hit him in January 1974, it did not depress him to the extent one would expect. To him it was almost a release and he was no longer divided trying to serve two worlds. He was now free from his dilemma and he could pursue his writing and religious activities without conflict. He rarely came to the Pottery because that depressed him, instead the potters visited him in the evenings. But I must say that up until a week before he died he occasionally said he had a dream of a pot that he wished he could have made before he lost his sight.'[19]

In 1977 a major retrospective exhibition was held at the Victoria and Albert Museum in honour of Bernard's ninetieth birthday. The display included 200 pots, with prints and drawings. The simple figurative motifs he used on his pots were the willow, the Tree of Life, bird, fish or hare, a leaf, various patterns and the human figure, usually against an Oriental background. All were loosely drawn with brush, comb, or tools he made himself from bamboo. Many of Bernard's home-made tools are still in use at the Leach Pottery. A book commemorating the V & A retrospective was edited by Carol Hogben, who worked there and curated the exhibition. In her introduction to *The Art of Bernard Leach* she writes, 'There is room, of course, for an infinite number of opinions as to who is the finest potter of our age. But there cannot be two views as to which has had the greatest influences on others.' Sadly, on Bernard's ninetieth birthday, his great friend, Shoji Hamada died. He had paid his last visit to St Ives in 1973.

DEATH OF BERNARD LEACH

Bernard died in 1979. Alice Moore, known for her embroidery, recalled that fateful day: 'I was with Bernard when he died. It just happened. When I had a stroke he came to see me and I was very fond of him. When he was in hospital at Hayle I used to take him little tiny wild flowers from my garden because he liked to have them near him on his table, but he couldn't see them because he was blind. When he was dying Eleanor, his daughter, rang and said would I go and see him with her and pick some flowers from the garden. Bernard was lying on his back on a couch. We started talking about where we were born. All this talk stirred old memories for Bernard of his first wife and the early years, but very soon he became agitated and the nurse said she would get him into bed. Eleanor and I waited outside. Within a few minutes he had died.'

After Bernard's death Janet decided to concentrate on her own work, not to take students and to cease the production of standard ware. A separate showroom was set aside for Bernard's work. Visitors travel from all over the

Visitors to the Leach Pottery in 1995: on the left are writer Eric Quayle, Seiji Oshima, director of the Setayaga Art Museum, Tokyo and Tomoo Hamada, with other Mashiko delegates.

Patrick Heron at his St Ives studio with Imi Arimoto, intepreter for the Mashiko delegation.

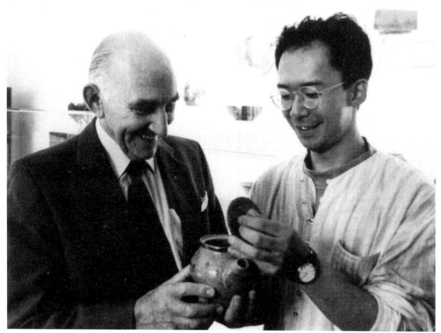

David Leach and Tomoo Hamada at Dartington in 1995 handling a pot made by Shoji at the Dartington Conference in 1952.

Tomoo visiting the Leach Pottery in 1995, sitting by the fireplace where grandfather Shoji cooked his meals in 1920.

The Bernard Leach showroom at the pottery.

David Leach's showroom at Lowerdown Pottery, Bovey Tracey, Devon, 1995.

world, especially Japan, to see where Bernard Leach and Shoji Hamada founded a pottery and an ideal way of working that built an enduring friendship and understanding between East and West. The Leach Pottery remains the Mecca for masters, students, admirers and collectors of pottery. Paul Rice, in his book *British Studio Ceramics in the 20th Century*, wrote: 'A good number of excellent potters worked at St Ives ... The mark they have left on the development of British studio ceramics cannot be erased.'

Early in 1995 the Nihon Mingeikan in Japan showed an exhibition entitled 'Bernard Leach and his Friends'. This same year ten delegates from the village of Mashiko visited Cornwall to view the Leach Pottery, Tate Gallery at St Ives and the Wingfield Digby collection of mainly Leach and Hamada pots; they were celebrating 75 years since Hamada's arrival in St Ives to establish the now famous pottery with Leach. Among the group was Tomoo, the son of Shinsaku and grandson of Hamada, carrying on the pottery tradition at Mashiko. While in St Ives Tomoo said the town was a place to fall in love with.

The Leach Pottery, no longer supporting a team of potters or producing a range of standard ware with a catalogue, quietly accepts that it still attracts students of pottery and admirers of the Leach tradition. The showroom displays the work of Janet Leach and Trevor Corser – not, it is hoped, the last of the potters to grace the workshop. Countless admirers of Bernard Leach and all he represented will be hoping for a renaissance.

Janet Leach in 1994, with favourite pots, Barbara Hepworth sculpture and painting by Kate Nicholson.

Bernard Howell Leach CBE

Born: Hong Kong 1887-1979
Studied: Slade School of Art and
London School of Art
Leach Pottery: 1920-1979
Lived/worked in St Ives, Cornwall, UK

'Potting is one of the few activities today in which a person can use his natural faculties of head, heart, and hand in balance.'

Bernard Leach at Mashiko Pottery, Japan in 1953.

Bernard Leach, the son of English parents, was born in Hong Kong, and lived also in Japan and Singapore, until sent to Beaumont Jesuit School in Windsor, England, at the age of ten. In 1903 he entered the Slade School of Art and studied drawing under Henry Tonks. After an abortive attempt to work in a bank he returned to college to study etching under Frank Brangwyn at the London School of Art where, at the age of sixteen, he was the youngest student.

In 1909 he returned to Japan taking with him an etching press, and introduced the technique of etching into that culture. It was in Japan, at a raku party with his friend Soetsu Yanagi, that he decorated his first pot. When he held it in his hands he realised, 'I have got to do this.' In 'An English Artist in Japan in 1920', Yanagi stated that there are few people who are able to live in the spirit of Japan - Leach was such a man. He very successfully spanned two cultures and was the first artist educated in the West to learn the techniques of Oriental pottery.

Leach studied under the potter Ogata Kenzan with fellow pupil Kenkichi Tomimoto. Kenzan was sixth in line of a family of master potters dating back to the seventeeth century. Leach learned his 'alphabet of clay' sitting on a hard floor, turning a Japanese potter's wheel with a stick. Leach and Tomimoto jointly inherited the title of Kenzan VII. A title, with the master's *Densho*

Part coffee set, speckled brown unglazed body c. 1956.

Stoneware vase decorated with sgraffito tree pattern on speckled grey ground. 42 cm high 1969.

(pottery glazes and recipes) was usually passed to a son, but being without a son Kenzan was happy to leave two pupils his title and techniques. With Kenzan's help Leach set up his first workshop and kiln in his garden.

In 1917 Leach was invited to build a pottery at Abiko, the home of Yanagi. It was here that Hamada wrote asking if he might meet Leach, whose pots he had admired while studying ceramics and glazing at technical college. Hamada wanted to learn more of the art of potting and Leach required the technical ability of Hamada's experience of glazes. Leach, Hamada and Yanagi formed a lifelong friendship.

Bernard Leach revived the art of hand craft pottery which was traditional in England before industrialisation. He spent his life learning what it meant to be a potter, and passed on his learning to his students. He probably created more potters than any other person, by his teaching, influence, writing, and his philosophy. The Leach tradition in craftsmanship and aesthetics is spread world wide. Emmanuel Cooper expressed the view that Bernard Leach was the outstanding leader of the studio pottery movement.

Bernard said there was an appropriateness in the parts of a pot, the foot, the belly, the neck, the shoulder. 'The form is the primary thing, texture, colour, pattern are secondary to the form, these are orchestration.

Tenmoku vase.

Pilgrim bottle. Stoneware decorated with incised bird on speckled buff surface. 32.5 cm high c. 1957.

The pot itself is the melody. The technique of learning to be a potter and to cover all the things involved, painting, sculpture, fine art, chemistry, geology, business, all these things are necessary. It's a very varied life.' [20] The decorative skills employed by Leach show a mastery of techniques through patterning of every kind, to figurative themes of animal forms, to the willow tree and pilgrim plates.

Among his many writings on ceramics, A Potter's Book has been the most influential and inspirational. In the chapter 'Towards A Standard' he says that 'pots, like all other forms of art, are human expressions: pleasure, pain or indifference before them depends upon their natures, and their natures are inevitably projec-

tions of the minds of their creators.'

Among the many honours bestowed on Bernard Leach were, in 1961, Honorary Doctorates in Literature from the University of Exeter and from Leeds University. One year later he was awarded the CBE (Commander of the British Empire). In Japan in 1966 he achieved the Order of the Sacred Treasure, second class, the highest award given to a foreigner. In 1968 the Freedom of the Borough of St Ives, also granted to Barbara Hepworth and Ben Nicholson, recognized an international contribution to the arts. He was honoured by the World Crafts Council in 1970 and was made a CH (Companion of Honour) in 1973.

Shoji Hamada

Born: Mizonokuchi, Kawasaki City,
Tokyo 1894-1978
Studied: Tokyo Technical College
Leach Pottery: 1920-1923
Lived/worked in Mashiko, Japan

'I think my experience in St Ives was invaluable. No matter where you are, experience must come to you. To know I was on the other side of the earth had a special meaning.'

Shoji Hamada at Mashiko Pottery, Japan in 1954.

Shoji Hamada was not born into a craftsman's household and had no tradition to copy. He therefore had freedom to embrace the crafts and pottery of Britain, using his knowledge of glaze chemistry learnt in Japan, and adopting English slipware. He was inspired by a small pitcher made by Leach and changed his studies from painting to ceramics. Their first meeting at Abiko, in Japan, grew into a lasting friendship. Shoji studied ceramics at Tokyo Technical College but felt his learning had very little to do with pottery techniques. He travelled to Cornwall with Bernard Leach in 1920 to set up the St Ives Pottery, building a Japanese three-chambered climbing kiln, the first to be installed in Britain. He also brought with him his traditional Japanese potter's wheel turned with a stick, because he was not experienced in operating any other kind of wheel. In this small fishing town Hamada began his life's work.

In the early days of the pottery a great deal was lost in the firing, but they experimented and learned from their experiences. They also competed to see who could throw the biggest pot. By the time Hamada left St Ives many technical problems had been solved and he had held several exhibitions in London, the last in Bond Street, where he sold all but three pieces.

Hamada took up residence in the

Rice ash pot. (Janet Leach collection)

Vase, painted sugar cane decoration incised through white ground. 30 cm high 1925.

St Ives Pottery and built his bed from the same wood that was used to fire the kiln. It was the only timber available. The design was based on an Elizabethan four-poster bed at Pendeen Manor house in Cornwall. He also fell in love with English Windsor and rush-bottomed chairs, and added many to his collection of furniture. After Hamada and Yanagi visited Britain in 1929, they returned to Japan 'richer by 300 chairs'. In 1974 Hamada commemorated his 80th birthday by donating his personal collection of paintings, glass, fabrics and objects from many countries, to the Mashiko Reference Collection Museum, which he had founded for the benefit of the public.

When Hamada returned to Japan from St Ives in 1923 he set up his workshop at Mashiko in the company of rural potters. He was attracted to the region by seeing a teapot made in that village, today known as Mingei, the folk craft village. When he left Cornwall he also left behind his pottery seal and said, 'I now think it is unnecessary to put your seal or stamp on your work.' He believed that the identity of the artist should show itself in the work, reflecting the Japanese philosophy that beauty is related to humility. Hamada did not want people to judge a pot by a signature and was concerned with the 'good pot' not with his own personality. Many of his pieces are recognis-

Dish. 28 cm x 28 cm 1940.

Slab pot, wax resist pattern, kaki iron glaze. 24.5 cm high 1960.

able by his characteristic brush marks of a stem-leaf motif.

In Mashiko Hamada found natural clays with good plasticity and ash and stone for glazes. He worked with the simplest of materials, using hairs from local dogs for his brushes and practised a philosophy of producing first class work from impure natural materials. 'Mr Hamada feels that the good pot is the result of the naturalness and flow that come only from making many pots. It's like practising scales. If you make 50 pots, the last is apt to be the best.'[21]

'Mashiko was a traditional pottery village. The potters made kitchen ware for Tokyo. Hamada transformed some of their traditional glazes such as kaki into an art form. After the war Mashiko had hard times due to the introduction of plastic, and the sale of processed food. The potters, seeing Hamada on the hill getting famous, began to do a Hamada-type domestic ware, and other potters moved into the area.'[22]

Many kilns have now been established in Mashiko and the village attracts many visitors. When Hamada, in 1975, was asked how he maintained his level of work he said: 'I feel now at my age my pots are better than when I was younger. Throwing, painting, pattern, all these techniques are quite natural to me and I can use them at will.'[23]

David Leach OBE

Born: Tokyo, Japan 1911
Studied: North Staffs Technical
College, Stoke-on-Trent
Leach Pottery: 1930-1955
Lives/works in Bovey Tracey,
Devon, UK

*'My father's work and thinking were
always in demand. I wanted to see his
work which I loved, helped in any way
I could. The team had its artistic director
in Bernard. My own development
could wait.'*

David Leach at St Ives Pottery, c.1940.

David Leach had his first pottery lessons as a boy from Hamada. At the age of 19, he joined his father at the Leach Pottery. There, he realised a growing and instinctive appreciation of the unique importance of his father's work as an artist and of his need for support at the pottery on practical, technical and economic levels. In 1934, David went to college in the heart of the Potteries, where he attended a technical and managerial course to the advantage of the Leach Pottery.

He was not motivated by any personal creative need but acquired the necessary skills, learning from other students, such as Muriel Bell and Charlotte Epton, as well as from his father. In later years he benefited by example from Harry Davis who was an exceptionally skilled maker. In retrospect David recognises that he was slow perhaps in not creating work on his own initiative, but he was never in conflict with his father's ideals and enjoyed a fond working relationship with Bernard for 25 years.

In 1953 he was invited by the principal of Loughborough College of Art, Leicester, to head the Ceramics Department for a year. This forced upon him a need to make decisions, both in his role as teacher and in

Teapot, porcelain with fluted decoration, pale celadon glaze. 1990. (photography: *Ceramic Review*)

Lidded spiral, brush decorated grey jar. 20 cm high 1994.

reliance upon his own aesthetic judgment, which effectively made him more self sufficient.

In 1955 David relinquished his responsibilities with the Leach Pottery and moved with his family to Lowerdown Pottery at Bovey Tracey, Devon. It was time to have a life of his own, be his own master, and pass on his considerable knowledge. He was an inspired teacher and among his many students were his sons John, Jeremy and Simon. He made slipware for four years before changing to stoneware. David also developed delicate porcelain with hand carving, and pale green celadon glaze which

the Sung dynasty Chinese potters had likened to 'sky after rain'.

William Ismay, a leading collector and critic, speaking at an exhibition of 'Three Generations of Leach' at the New Ashgate Gallery in 1986 said: 'His cut flutings on pots of essentially twentieth-century feel are among the most sensitive done by anyone since the technique was classically developed by Oriental potters.' He is a meticulous potter, which is one reason for using porcelain. It is technically exacting to keep the shape of a delicate and semi-transparent object which has be to thrown carefully and thinly.

Willow design vase. 20 cm high.

Fluted, lidded tenmoku jar. 28 cm high 1994.

David is basically concerned with form made on the wheel in the first instance. His inspiration and thinking often come directly through working on the wheel with the clay flowing through his fingers. At 85 he still pots, has a showroom, teaches, accepts invitations to exhibit his work, lectures, demonstrates, travels widely, assesses at various colleges, and is active in the Devon Guild of Craftsmen. He was awarded an OBE (Order of the British Empire) for services to ceramics in 1987. He says he will continue with his life as a potter until his health gives out. He would also like to continue the things his father started – and get down to the written word.

At Lowerdown he makes his own tools from metal, wood or bamboo; only teapot hole borers or drills are bought. He uses both kick- and power-wheels. Of his work as a potter he says: 'I have studied and learned the drill of function so that I don't have to think about it any more. It does not occupy my conscious mind which is on qualitative things, shape, glaze, decoration.'

Janet Leach

Born: Texas, USA 1918
Studied: Inwood Pottery and Alfred
University
Leach Pottery: 1956 to present day
Lives/works in St Ives, Cornwall, UK

*'I didn't come to Cornwall as a student
of Bernard's. I was a potter in my own
right. I had my own ideas. I came to
marry him .'*

Janet Leach with pots, c.1985.

Janet Leach (Darnell) as a young woman studied sculpture in New York. She worked as a sculptor's assistant on the Federal Art Project, set up to provide employment for artists, but it became obvious that a woman sculptor would run into difficulties trying to get commissions. During two years of the war she worked as a welder on naval warships, and afterwards studied ceramics at the Inwood Pottery and Alfred University. In 1947 she left New York City to start a pottery at Threefold Farm, Spring Valley, 25 miles north of the city where an artists' centre had been established for many years. At this time she was feeling dissatisfied with her work, defeated in her attempt to find the secret of making a good pot.

She became interested in the philosophy and techniques of Japanese pottery after meeting Bernard Leach, Shoji Hamada and Soetsu Yanagi at Black Mountain College, when they toured and lectured in America in 1952, immediately following the Dartington International Conference of Potters and Weavers. She was inspired by their commitment and love of the craft, and Hamada's flowing rhythms on the wheel, confirming his philosophy of simplicity and honesty. Through Bernard's intro-

Wood-fired stoneware. 18 cm high.

Black clay, white glaze poured decoration.

Black stoneware clay, white glaze poured decoration.

duction she was able to study with Hamada in Japan for two years.

In 1954 Janet was the first foreign woman to study pottery in Japan – in Mashiko – and the only woman in Japan to be seen working on the potter's wheel. After six months in Mashiko Hamada advised her to study in the traditional country potteries. In the mountain village of Tamba, while living and working in the family pottery of Tanso Ichino, she did most of her serious potting. In turn, in 1969, she was to invite Shigeyoshi, the son of the Ichino family, to work at the Leach pottery.

Making the most of her opportunities and experience Janet travelled widely, visiting the many folkcraft potteries, often with Hamada and Bernard. She met Bernard's friends, including Kenkichi Tomimoto and Kanjiro Kawai. She had the constant advice of Shoji Hamada during her time in Japan. She considers him her mentor: 'It was as a potter in Japan that I really started making decent pots. I think my pots matured in Japan. I have done a lot of experiments in clay bodies. I like clay bodies rather than glazes.' Many of her pots are only slightly glazed. Janet came to St Ives in 1956 to marry Bernard Leach. She found the stones, textures

Cut-sided black stoneware pot, unglazed.

and granite walls of Cornwall 'very exciting' and they greatly influenced her work. Bernard had a high regard for her individual style.

'I have always been an advocate of natural materials as much as possible, but I am not one of those who digs one's own clay. I think machinery has its place in our life as twentieth-century potters and I am pleased that our standard body at the Leach Pottery is half natural "as dug" clay.' Janet's plea to the young potters of today is for a primary and simple approach to all the techniques involved in potting and advises that no amount of ingenious tools and mechanical knick-knacks will contribute to the making of a good pot.

Although she studied sculpture and pottery she never mixed the two: 'each has its own standard.' Like many artists and craftsmen she cannot imagine retiring. The lower room at the cottage is filled with pots which she admires, many of them made with the inspired hands of Shoji Hamada. A large 400-year old Tamba pot is placed so that it is the first object to meet her eye when she wakes in the morning.

RICHARD BATTERHAM   Lidded jar 14.5 cm high. Brushed with thick china clay slip, and salt glazed. c.1977.(Photography: Peter Kinnear, from *Bernard Leach, Hamada and their Circle*, Tony Birks and Cornelia Wingfield Digby)

Plate 1

JOHN BEDDING   Raku bowl 25 cm high. 1994.

Plate 2

MICHAEL CARDEW   Vase. 48 cm high. c.1937. (photography: Duncan Painter/Wenford Bridge Pottery)

Plate 3

TREVOR CORSER   Stoneware bottle with lugs, Hakeme glaze. 50 cm high.1994.(Photography: Ron Sutherland)

BERNARD FORRESTER
Stoneware vase with lustre gold decoration. 27 cm high. 1988.

CECIL BAUGH   Egyptian blue earthenware pot.

Plates 4,5,6

VALENTINOS CHARALAMBOUS   Earthenware bowl. 45 cm diameter.

Plate 7

SHOJI HAMADA   Late pot. 19.5 cm high. 1970. (collection: Janet Leach)

Plate 8

GWYN HANSSEN PIGOTT   Wood-fired porcelain. 1992. (photography: Michael Holohan)

MICHAEL LEACH   Earthenware jar, with various slip decoration. 29 cm high.

ANNE KJAERSGAARD   Pot. 25 cm high.

Plates 9,10,11

SHIGEYOSHI ICHINO   Plate with trailed glaze. 55.5 cm diameter.

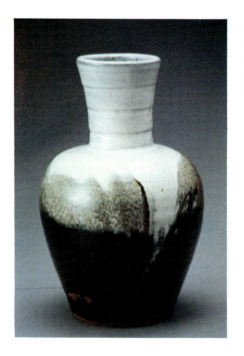

SHINSAKU HAMADA
Baluster vase, con-
centric incised circles,
overlapped white and
black glaze.

Plates 12,13

BERNARD LEACH   Stoneware vase, brown on oatmeal glaze. 31.8 cm high. 1946.

Plate 14

DAVID LEACH   Faceted jar with poured overlapping glazes. 1990. (photography: *Ceramic Review*)

Plate 15

JOHN LEACH   Ash glazed bottles. 27 cm, 16 cm and 12.5 cm high. 1995.
(photography: Peter Atherton-Galbraith)

Plate 16

JANET LEACH   Ash glazed stoneware pot. (photography: Peter Kinnear/Leach Pottery)

Plate 17

WARREN MACKENZIE   Stoneware vase. 28 cm high. 1979.

Plate 18

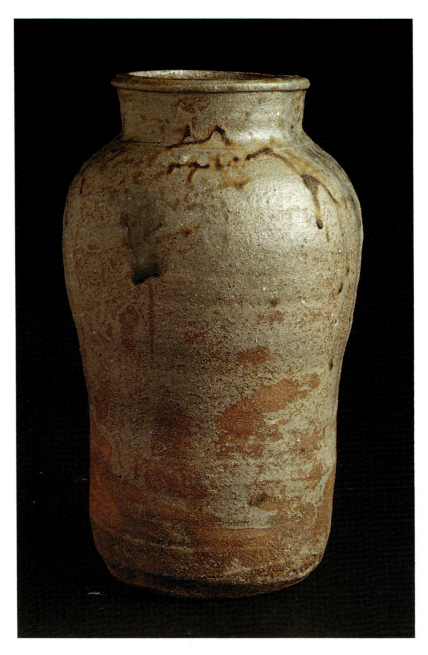

WILLIAM MARSHALL   Stoneware jar, raw glazed, with thin ash glaze on
shoulder and inside. c.1973.(photography: Peter Kinnear, from *Bernard
Leach, Hamada and their Circle*, Tony Birks and Cornelia Wingfield Digby)

Plate 19

BYRON TEMPLE   Tie box. 15 cm high. 1986.

Plate 20

JEFF OESTREICH   Beaked pitchers, salt-fired, thrown and altered. 18 cm high.

JASON WASON   Raku vessel, saturated with copper. 50 cm high.

Plates 21,22

POTTERS
Batterham
to
Zadek

Richard Batterham

Born: 1936
Studied: Bryanston Public School
Leach Pottery: 1957-1958
Lives/works in Blandford, Dorset, UK

'Batterham has always known where he was going and by the time he left St Ives he had planned his future in some detail.' Muriel Rose

Dinah Dunn (Batterham) 1954.

Richard Batterham showed an interest in pottery from an early age and was fortunate to attend Bryanston School where boys were encouraged to learn about the craft. The school workshop was run by Donald Potter who gave the pupils time to practise their skills on the wheel and learn how to master the wood-fired kiln. This early learning was a distinct advantage when he applied to work at the Leach Pottery.

During his year of study at the Leach Pottery, he was fortunate to meet Atsuya Hamada, the son of

Shoji, who was on a visit from Japan and was furthering his studies at St Ives. Working on the permanent staff of the pottery was Dinah Dunn, who trained at Hull College of Art, Yorkshire and spent about five years at the St Ives Pottery. She later married Richard, giving up her own interest in ceramics to look after their large family of children.

Working at the pottery helped further Richard's ambition to be a potter in his own right and, after leaving St Ives, he and his wife bought a cottage in Durweston, near

Batterham tea pots.

Blandford in Dorset. He built an oil-fired two-chambered climbing kiln and began potting straight away. He produced well designed stoneware of a domestic type on a small scale until, after six years, he completed the building for a larger workshop close to home and was able to extend his range of pots.

Richard Batterham is regarded by many as one of the finest makers of domestic stoneware in the Leach tradition. Although he remains true to his intention of making pots that 'enrich rather than adorn life', he has extended his range and produced pots that are not just strictly useful. The designs are semi-matt celadons with minimal decoration. He works entirely alone at his craft, firing the kiln five or six times a year. The design is based on a Japanese climbing kiln similar to that at the Leach Pottery.

'As in all the making and firing, preconceptions must be forgotten, and an open mind kept, able to receive the good unknown qualities which will appear. One must not dictate, but listen, observe and respond.' [24]

Cecil Baugh OD

Born: Portland, Jamaica, West
Indies 1908
Studied: British Council Scholarship
Leach Pottery: 1948-1950
Lives/works in Kingston, Jamaica

*'My experience at the Leach Pottery was
tremendous; it enabled me to take back
to my home in Jamaica the potter's art
in its true form.'*

Cecil Baugh in Jamaica 1991.

Cecil Baugh, as a young man, was influenced by African women potters who made low-fired earthenware pots. After working at the Leach Pottery he returned home and built a studio in Kingston, Jamaica. He was now experienced in the process of making and firing earthenware and stoneware clays. In 1950 he had his first one-man exhibition where he showed, amongst others, a stoneware pot made and fired while at the Leach Pottery. This exposed a new technique to Jamaica.

His stay in England was a round of experiences. He worked for three months with Margaret Leach, a former student of Bernard's, at the Barn Pottery in the Wye Valley. He visited Stoke-on-Trent to experience mass production wares. He also met Michael Cardew and helped solve problems of porous clay with David Leach. While at Dartington Pottery, he demonstrated the Jamaican free-form technique.

He has trained many students and was Head of Ceramics at the Jamaica School of Art. His current work is mainly stoneware, although he also works in earthenware. He is currently undertaking research on shales

Stoneware vase 'Rainbow'. 40cm high.

which have been collected locally from the foot of a mountain. He also developed a Hope slip glaze, so named after the Hope River. This river-bed material produced an ash mottled yellow glaze.

In 1953 on the first visit of the Queen to Jamaica, Lady Foot, wife of the Governor of Jamaica, presented one of Cecil's pots to Her Majesty. She has now received four of his pieces. Works have also been officially presented to the Emperor of Japan, Pope John Paul II, and President Nelson Mandela.

Cecil helped to establish the first visual arts training institution in the English-speaking Caribbean, along with artists in graphic design, painting and furniture. He has received many honours for his work in ceramics. In 1975 the Government of Jamaica awarded him the Order of Distinction. In 1984 he received the Gold Musgrave Award for his book *Baugh, Jamaica's Master Potter*. In 1991 the National Gallery of Jamaica opened the Cecil Baugh Gallery of Ceramics as part of the development of the visual arts on the island.

John Bedding

Born: London 1947
Studied: Sir John Cass School
of Art, London
Leach Pottery: 1969-1971
& 1973-1979
Lives/works in St Ives, Cornwall, UK

'Bernard's biggest influence was his philosophy. He was around for my first two years. Bill Marshall was the main influence for the shape of pots. Janet looked with a sculptor's eye.'

John Bedding at St Ives Pottery Gallery in 1995.

John Bedding worked for a year with Jean Tessier at his atelier in Villenaux, France, after his apprenticeship at the Leach Pottery. He was joined there by Shigeyoshi Ichino, who had worked with him at the Leach. In 1973 John joined the Leach permanent staff and produced standard ware as well as developing his own style. 'The best heritage I have got from the Leach is an eye for shape.'

In 1979 he was invited to work for the Ichino family pottery in Tachiqui, Japan, a village in the centre of Tamba, an ancient pottery area, where they still used wood-fired dragon kilns. That year in Japan was completed with a successful one-man exhibition in Osaka. After a tour of the East he returned to St Ives and in 1982 organised his first workshop in Penzance, Cornwall. In 1984 he made a conscious decision to distance himself from the Leach and Japanese influences, although he loves and admires traditional pots, and admits that the experiences of the St Ives Pottery, and craft life in Japan, will be long lasting.

John's pots are raku-fired. His is a very western approach. He is interested in the accidental and natural

Raku bottle 51cm high 1994.

chemistry of raku firing, but also in developing his own individual techniques which require timing and critical judgment. He works with copper and silver nitrate glazes with contrasting unglazed burnished surfaces. He has never lost the way to explore which he learnt at the Leach Pottery, where the approach was to discover source materials using natural elements rather than ready-made glazes and pigments. 'It was a fantastic background for the craft of making a pot and developing your own individual style.'

In 1990 John moved his workshop and gallery to Fish Street, St Ives, with a showcase for his work and for other potters he admires. He continues to work with raku, finding techniques which enable him to explore more closely the relationship of pottery to the natural world. He has also revived the domestic stoneware range of earlier years. He has built links with the painters and sculptors who work close by, especially those exploring surface area and the geology of West Penwith, Cornwall.

Valerie Bond

Born: Croydon, Surrey 1923
Studied: Bromley School of Art,
Kent, Royal College of Art, London
Leach Pottery: 1945-1946
Lives/works in Bridport, Dorset, UK

*'There really was a very good team spirit
and Bernard was very kind. David was a
very good and patient teacher.'*

Valerie Bond at Leach Pottery, St Ives in 1946.

Valerie Bond arrived at the Leach Pottery in 1945 after a chance encounter with Mariel Cardew, wife of Michael, who gave her an introduction to Bernard. She had spent four years as an art student at Bromley School of Art and worked on the land during the war. On her arrival at the pottery David Leach came out of the army, Horatio Dunn from the navy, and Kenneth Quick began work as an apprentice. On the staff were Aileen Newton, Mary Gibson-Horrocks and Margaret Leach.

The pottery team had lists of shapes to make for the week and things went fairly smoothly, she recalls, except for panics at the time of exhibitions. 'In making the standard ware we had to have the shape exactly right, or it would be thrown away. Bernard drew each shape and we studied them before we made them. Handles had to "grow" like a tree, beakers had to "spring" and have an imaginary circle inside them. Knobs had to be easy to "hold", feet were finished and turned at an angle to '"flow" into the pots, and jugs had to "pour" well.'

Enthusiasm for work and play was overwhelming; swimming, walking

Slipware dish burnished with a pebble 1950.

and cycling were part of the routine. At 11am everyone stopped for breakfast round the fire and Kenneth Quick made toast, spread with peanut butter. In the winter kneading had to be done outside and knuckles had permanent chilblains from the icy clay.

In 1946 Valerie studied sculpture at the Royal College of Art under Frank Dobson and John Skeaping. Later she taught pottery at Camberwell School of Art, married, and became Mrs Prescott. At a studio in Kensington she began making shapes based on primitive birds of many different designs and was encouraged by Hans Coper, who saw them in the Berkeley Gallery. Photographs of them were exhibited in London during the Festival of Britain in 1951. For the last 25 years she has been engaged in wood engravings, and drawing for *The Countryman*.

To celebrate the 50th anniversary of Valerie's first day at the Leach Pottery, John and Lizzie Leach held a firing at Mulchelney Pottery in Somerset. Elizabeth and David Leach and friends came, and Valerie helped stoke the kiln.

Ian Box

Born: Fulham, London 1949
Studied: Cornwall College, Ceramics
Leach Pottery: 1974-1975
Lives/works in Sennen, Cornwall, UK

'The experience of working at the Leach Pottery was of enormous benefit to me. At first I felt overawed by the high standard of work, but the camaraderie of my workmates soon put me at ease.'

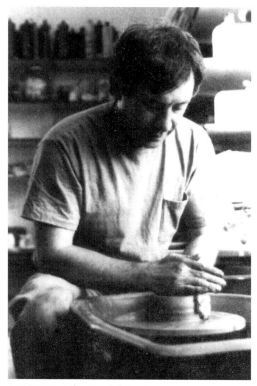

Ian Box at John Daniel Centre.

Ian Box moved to Cornwall in 1957 with his mother and twin brother. In 1972 with his wife and brother, he studied ceramics at Cornwall College under Roger Veal and David Metcalfe. William Marshall was introduced in 1973 to teach throwing techniques and Janet Leach was the course advisor. On seeing his diploma presentation Janet invited him to work for her at the Leach Pottery. He also gained Licentiate acceptance of the Society of Industrial Artists and Designers.

Bill Marshall's enthusiasm and love of pottery were an inspiration. Ian found the potters working at Leach – Trevor Corser, John Bedding, John Reeve and Mick Cartwright – extremely capable and immersed himself in the task of becoming as able as them. His throwing technique improved considerably. 'The experience gave me the precious gifts of enthusiasm and confidence in my ability and for that I am very grateful.' Janet worked at her wheel in the pottery cottage but was in regular contact. 'She was very aware of my progress, guiding me where

Collection of stoneware items.

she could.'

After leaving the Leach Pottery he and his wife started the Trevillian Pottery in Penzance. After five years, he then worked as a technician at Falmouth School of Art and finally in 1984 became a Day Care Officer at the John Daniel Centre, in Penzance, where he teaches pottery and social skills to people with learning difficulties. He works with low-fired terracotta ware, which students can decorate.

Ian is now building a kiln at home to resume making stoneware. 'My style is very much in the Leach mould, that is an East/West meeting of traditions. The work of the potter is both a mental and a spiritual process; to succeed one must have love and determination. I have never stopped learning or enjoying the many changes of teaching.' On occasions Ian and his wife visited Bernard at his flat. 'He was ninety, and blind, but still his mind was young. He loved to feel pots and talk about them.'

Norah Braden

Born: 1901
Studied: Royal College of Art
Leach Pottery: 1924-1927
Lives in Sussex, UK

'Norah was perhaps the most sensitive of all the students who have spent time at the Pottery.' Bernard Leach

Norah Braden at Coleshill Pottery, Berkshire.

Norah Braden studied painting at the Royal College of Art but switched to pottery under William Staite Murray. However, wanting to increase her knowledge and experience of studio pottery, she arrived at the Leach Pottery on the recommendation of Sir William Rothenstein, who said, 'I am sending you a genius.' She had been inspired by Leach's work which she saw in an exhibition in London and persuaded him to take her on as a student in St Ives. Her contemporaries at that time were Michael Cardew and Katharine Pleydell-Bouverie.

The 1920s were an experimental era for the establishment of hand-crafted pots. It was also unusual at the time for a woman to take up such a craft. Bernard Leach was barely able to make a living from his tableware of individually made bowls, cups and plates. He relied on his more expensive studio pots which he exhibited in London and Japan to provide an income. However, his three students flourished under his tuition.

Leach described Norah as one of the most gifted of potters. She was highly self-critical and because of Bernard's teaching of balance, the rim of the pot being right for the foot, and his belief in aesthetics, she

Stoneware jar, green grey, peat ash glaze with red brown iron splashes, pinkish body. 16cm high 1939.

became a hard judge of her efforts and destroyed much of her work. There is little evidence left of the pots she made in her time at the Leach Pottery although work is at Kettle's Yard, Cambridge and the Victoria and Albert Museum, London.

A firm friendship developed between Katharine Pleydell-Bouverie and Norah and in 1928, when Katharine set up a pottery on the family estate at Coleshill in Berkshire, Norah joined her. Together they worked on experimental glazes, using material gathered from the woods and surrounding countryside. The two potters exhibited their work at the Little Gallery, London in 1929 and in Bond Street in 1930. The latter exhibition was singled out for praise in *The Times*, an achievement in itself since it was then unusual for potters to command critical acclaim.

During school holidays she continued to work with Katharine at Kilmington Manor pottery. In the 1950s Norah, with the onset of arthritis, ceased potting. She taught at Brighton and Chichester Colleges of Art, Sussex, and at Camberwell School of Art, London. In 1994 her own collection of forty pots went on sale at Bonhams.

AB

Alan Brough

Born: Wilmslow, Cheshire, 1924
Studied: Camberwell School of
Arts and Crafts
Leach Pottery: 1968-1972
Lives/works in Newlyn, Cornwall UK

*'Bernard said that a good pot would
look equally well on an old piece of
furniture as it would on a modern
Swedish glass table.'*

Alan Brough at Newlyn workshop in 1995.

Alan Brough, already a very experienced potter, went to the Leach Pottery to help organise the students. Bill Marshall was working with Bernard, helping to throw his large pots because of his age, and Janet also wanted someone to organise the workshops. As well as doing this, Alan was making his own pots in his particular style and encouraging the students to find theirs.

When he left in 1972 he started the Alan Brough Pottery in nearby Newlyn, and was there for 18 years, making stoneware and porcelain.

'Now I am older I'm making earthenware. Bernard was a glaze man. I am a form and decorative man.' He used to dine with Bernard quite regularly and learned to listen and adapt, not to follow. He felt others made pale imitations of Leach pots and therefore failed to find themselves.

'Bernard made very important statements. He said, "If you want to make a soup bowl think soup."' If Alan makes a vessel for water or wine it will look right for the liquid it will hold. He learnt to think usefulness and suitability. 'Bernard pointed out

Earthenware teapot.

that if an Indian woman was going to make a bowl for wheat she would make a low shallow dish for that purpose. She would do it without intellectualising. He thought some of the best pots were made by women.'

Alan tells his students the potentialities of clay, which is for him the most important material in the world, encouraging them to explore the particular clay in their area and decide whether to study glazes, or make sculptural forms, or pure potter's forms for use. 'I wouldn't like to tell anybody what kind of pots to make.' He feels clay has become invisible because of its usefulness. Some of the history of the world is written on so-called stones, which were really clay slabs fired. He makes pots because he wants clay to be visible.

He has recently exhibited in France where he finds a great acceptance of red earthenware and a high regard and deep feeling for the craft of pottery. There he feels the craftsman is valued and enjoys a dignified status.

Tony Burgess

Tony Burgess in Australia.

Born: Ramsgate, Kent 1931
Studied: Travelled extensively
Europe, America
Leach Pottery: 1965-1967
Lives/works in New South Wales,
Australia

*'The experience of working at Leach has
stayed with me all these years.'*

Tony Burgess, after gaining experience by travelling in America, Canada and Mexico, returned to England in 1963 and helped John Reeve and Warren MacKenzie to start a pottery at Hennock in Devon. John Reeve had left the Leach Pottery in 1961 (but later returned) and Warren MacKenzie was on a year's sabbatical from America, having previously studied with Bernard from 1949 to 1952.

In 1965, on the recommendations of Reeve and MacKenzie, Tony began his training at the Leach Pottery. 'I remember clearly nights spent having dinner with Bernard overlooking Porthmeor beach, talking the night away – not just about pots. What a lovely, lovely man he was.' Tony remembers all those long nights firing the second chamber of the old climbing kiln, with Bill Marshall, 'the real backbone of the pottery'. It was John Reeve who first opened his eyes 'to see', and was a positive influence in his development as a potter. Other overseas companions were Susan Smith, Tim Stampton and Jorgen Jorgensen. The visit of Shoji Hamada

Jug, tenmoku and Cornish stone. 27cm high.

with his wife and daughter in 1966 was an inspiration to all those working at the St Ives Pottery at the time.

Whatever traumas were being experienced at the Leach Pottery –whether at a personal or professional level – the kiln always got fired every three weeks. Effort and commitment from everyone involved was the secret of the team's success.

After completing his training at St Ives, Tony emigrated to Australia in the late 1960s and started the Tarrawonga Pottery, Mittagong in New South Wales. He also managed the Sturt Pottery there for one year. After many years, and a series of major life threatening illnesses, he returned to the Sturt Pottery where he rents workshop space to make pots he can live with. He has abandoned the process of marking his pots with a seal or signature. Echoing Hamada, he says: 'My philosophy, if I have one, is that the work speaks for itself, that pots should be strong, generous, and full of life. That if they are not made with love, how can we expect others to love them?'

Michael Cardew CBE

Born: Wimbledon, Surrey 1901-1983
Studied: 'Greats' Oxford University
Leach Pottery: 1923-1926
Lived/worked in Bodmin,
Cornwall, UK

'What I learned from Leach was the supreme importance of shape and how much depends upon the subtle differences of form, even in such apparently simple things as plates and dishes.'

Michael Cardew at Wenford Bridge Pottery, Bodmin in 1967.

Michael Cardew shared with Bernard Leach a fascination for early English slipware. The lessons he learned as the first student at the St Ives Pottery helped build his personal philosophy. He was not interested in imitating the work of the master but acquired an aesthetic judgement that lasted a lifetime. 'There must have been a door marked 'Pottery' in my childhood, but I can't remember the exact moment when it opened.' [25]

He admired Hamada's pots and this influence was lasting. He thought Hamada was a magical man who made 'the most lovely raku out of red clay slipware', fired with raku glaze,

red clay dipped in white, sgraffito decoration with dashes of copper green.

His years at the Leach were formative, especially in conversations with Hamada, Matsubayashi and Norah Braden. He valued Bernard as a teacher, who was able to articulate what Michael had always known but for which he couldn't find words.

In 1926 Michael bought a derelict pottery at Winchcombe in Gloucestershire and established a rural workshop, reviving the English slipware tradition. In 1939 he left Winchcombe in the hands of Ray Finch, who had served an apprentice-

Earthenware jar, greenish yellow brown, decoration incised through light slip, red body. 48cm high.1937.

ship with him three years earlier, and moved to Cornwall where he set up the Wenford Bridge Pottery, near Bodmin, producing earthenware and stoneware.

Michael said of his hollow ware that he only ever made one pot and all that followed were a variation of that one. His plates and dishes were a great vehicle for his vigorous brush work or sgraffito decoration. His work was consistently at the English end of the bridge between East and West.

From 1942 to 1948 he was pottery instructor at Achimota College in Ghana, following on from former St Ives students Kenneth Murray and Harry Davis. Later, from 1951 to 1965, he worked in Ghana and Nigeria, introducing wheel-made pottery and stoneware to African pupils and developing his own range of work.

He returned to Wenford Bridge in 1965. His later years were spent making pots, writing, teaching and demonstrating. He toured America, Canada, Australia and New Zealand. His first book, *Pioneer Pottery* was published in 1969. His autobiography was completed in 1988 by his son Seth, who carries on the pottery at Wenford Bridge, marrying tradition with his own individual approach. Seth's son Ara is also a potter.

Michael Cartwright

Born: Sawston, South
Cambridgeshire, 1951
Studied: Farnham School of
Art, Ceramics
Leach Pottery: 1973-1975
Lives/works in Kingsbridge,
Devon, UK

*'Living and working with people for
whom pot making sustained their very
existence was a revelation. I loved every
minute of it and it changed my life.'*

**Michael Cartwright with pots by Bill Marshall
and Katharine Pleydell-Bouverie.**

Michael Cartwright had his first taste of ceramics on a Cambridge College of Arts and Technology foundation course. His lecturer, Zoe Ellison, inspired him sufficiently for him to change his course from painting to studying ceramics at Farnham College of Art, Surrey. On finishing his course the ultimate goal was to work at the Leach Pottery. Few workshops offered training or apprenticeships at that time.

He knew Cornwall quite well, having spent previous summers helping to fire Michael Cardew's kiln at Wenford Bridge. He approached Janet Leach but there were no places available. He then became a technician on the studio pottery course at Harrow School of Art, Middlesex, the year Mick Casson left. 'It was then that Shigeyoshi Ichino left the Leach Pottery and I was fortunate enough to be offered his place.' It was at St Ives that he felt he did his best work. He admires 'pots that are about weight, comfort and quietness whilst remaining strong and personal'.

After eighteen enjoyable months he prepared to set up his own pottery in Cambridgeshire. Spike Pottery, where he produced a standard ware

Bread crock, ash glaze. 44 cm high.

range and some individual pieces, was in existence for four years. He also lectured in ceramics. Whilst in St Ives he had taken to surfing and he now desperately missed the sea. He was fortunate to find a position in the Channel Islands, at the Guernsey Pottery, where he had the task of training a team of proficient throwers and to switch production from slip cast to thrown ware, and redesigning a stoneware and earthenware range.

In the 1980s Michael was diagnosed as having spinal problems and was uncertain about his long term health. A career change took him to Reading University to study as a secondary school teacher. On completion of his studies he took a job at Ivybridge Community College in South Devon, where he teaches 'A' level students. He has become an avid collector of studio pottery. 'I feel Bernard's concern with form, particularly in relation to standard ware, has not really been matched by many contemporary studio potters; decoration and effects have replaced this concern.'

Len Castle

Born: Auckland, New Zealand 1924
Studied: B.Sc. University of
New Zealand
Leach Pottery: 1956-1957
Lives/works in Auckland,
New Zealand

'I was loaned the only copy in New Zealand of A Potter's Book *by Bernard Leach. The chapter "Towards a Standard" engendered my philosophy about pottery as a means of expression'.*

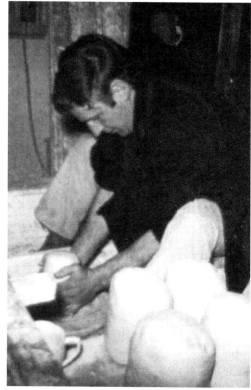

Len Castle at workshop, Titirangi, New Zealand in 1979.

Len Castle was introduced to pottery at the age of 10 when he watched a demonstration of pottery making, and a childhood discovery of clay at the beach influenced his development as a potter. The 1950s was a decade in which Len accumulated and synthesised many influences and developed a personal ceramic language. In 1956 a scholarship took him to Cornwall to study at the Leach Pottery, where he learnt a disciplined work pattern which enabled him to become a successful potter in his own right.

He studied the ceramic collections in England and was especially attracted to the pottery of ancient China, Korea and Japan, and the contemporary examples of Hamada's pots in the same tradition. Later, during Hamada's visit to New Zealand, he watched him demonstrating pots on the wheel, making fast intuitive decisions when the form of the pot was at its vital phase.

An Arts Council Fellowship-funded visit to Japan in 1966, where he was welcomed at the village of Mashiko, rekindled his friendship with Atsuya

Pouring bottle with loop handle. 1980s.

Hamada, with whom he had worked at the St Ives Pottery. He also visited the Kanjiro Kawai workshop in Kyoto where his pots were fired in a wood-fired multi-chambered climbing kiln. He returned frequently to Japan to study its many potteries.

During the past 32 years Len's workshops and showrooms have been associated with his various homes in Titirangi, where his pots share space with books, paintings, rock samples, fossils, minerals and crystals. His spirituality comes from a close and harmonious relationship with nature.

'Those of us who work with clay can be called alchemists and visual poets. We can set our language, cadences and stanzas in form, colour and texture. As alchemists we can coax magic from our seemingly inert clay. We can call on the flame to exert its power and show its fiery palette. We can call on seemingly inert materials to undergo transmutations. We can arrange a marriage of passion between intensely heated molecules. Their children will be colour and texture.'

Valentinos Charalambous

Born: Famagusta, Cyprus 1929
Studied: Central School of Arts
and Crafts, London
Leach Pottery: 1950-1951
Lives/works in Limassol and Nicosia

*'My work isn't directly influenced by
Bernard Leach but life is much richer for
having known him. Even now, I find
myself asking "what would BL have
thought of this?"'*

**Valentinos Charalambous at Nicosia exhibition,
Cyprus, 1996.**

Valentinos Charalambous was born into a family of traditional potters. To broaden his horizons, he studied under Dora Billington and Gilbert Harding-Green at the Central School in 1948. Leach's *A Potter's Book* was the 'Bible', and everyone's ambition was to work with the master. Valentinos wrote, giving his family credentials. BL replied: 'Come down. You are a potter's son, and one cannot be a potter without having the taste of clay as a young man.'

Along with other acolytes, Valentinos threw domestic pots to BL's designs, with a free day each week to create his own work. At the evening gatherings, Leach 'showed great humility, listening as well as talking, treating us as his equals.' But he was a stern judge and never held back in his comments. Of Valentinos' pots, he once said: 'Your form is good, but you decorate like a dancer who has lost his rhythm.'

Back in Cyprus, Valentinos immersed himself in his national culture. 'Bernard represented understatement; in the Middle East, we overstate.' The family had borrowed to send Valentinos to London and to repay the bank, he found himself artistically compromised, forced to produce and sell overly commercial

Unglazed ceramic sculpture. 105cm.

work – mainly to British service families on the island.

Artistic salvation was round the corner, when Valentinos was invited by the Iraqi Ministry of Education to establish a Department of Ceramics at the Institute of Fine Arts in Baghdad. His subsequent life's work in education and cultural relations in the Middle East and Cyprus has meant that, without commercial pressure, his own creative work could develop with integrity.

A major exhibition in Nicosia in 1996 confirmed Valentinos' stature as a master artist. The work on show was redolent of Greek and Middle East traditions, with exquisitely decorated bowls and dishes alongside huge ceramic sculptures. 'My work, whether ceramic sculpture, murals, or simple domestic ware, is the synthesis of emotional artistic experiences and exposure to other cultures over many years.'

Dora Billington once wrote that Valentinos' 'individuality and unwillingness to go along with the international stream is truly of value today, when contemporary idioms in all the arts are inclined to be the same all the world over.'

TC:

Trevor Corser

Born: Oldham 1938
Studied: Apprentice at Leach
Leach Pottery: 1966 to present day
Lives/works in St Ives, Cornwall, UK

'Without those years of making standard ware I would not have achieved the skill I now have. It became a natural ability to make and apply the right handle to a pot.'

Trevor Corser at Leach Pottery, St Ives in 1995.

Trevor Corser combined his work of diving for crayfish and lobsters with jobs as a casual labourer at the Leach Pottery when the weather was bad. He mixed clay and stacked the kiln, packed the pots and learned various skills from everybody working there. As he acquired experience he became more interested in pottery than fishing and eventually began working full time. While still carrying out the basic tasks, he learned the techniques of coiling, to throwing on the wheel, with the expert guidance of Bill Marshall, Janet and Bernard Leach, until he emerged as a craftsman.

After Bernard's death, Janet gradually dispensed with the responsibilities of taking on students and supervising the production of standard ware. Staffing levels were reduced as potters left to set up on their own, until only Trevor and Janet remained to carry on the working life of the pottery. He occupies the workshop, whilst Janet has her wheel in the cottage. He still mixes the glazes

Pitcher, tenmoku glaze, fluted decoration. 48 cm high 1995.

from powder and experiments with ash glazes and colours. The clay is hand wedged, 'a kind of kneading to remove the air pockets'. He enjoys the whole process of working with clay and handling pots, packs and fires the kiln and looks forward to the magical moment of opening the kiln door after a firing to experience the end result. He is also responsible for the plant maintenance.

'I still use the wooden kick wheel made in the 1930s by Dicon Nance, the local furniture maker, and Bernard's tools. I make various tools for use in decoration from bundles of bamboo, brought by visiting Japanese potters.' They also bring gifts of brushes.

A constant stream of visitors come from all over the world to see the historic collection of Leach and Hamada pots and to buy the present-day work of Trevor and Janet from the pottery showroom. Trevor was the first potter invited to provide 'pots in use' for the Tate Gallery, St Ives, when it opened in 1993.

Harry Davis
May Davis 1914-1995

Born: Cardiff 1910-1986
Studied: Art
Leach Pottery: 1933-1937
Lived/worked mainly in Nelson,
New Zealand

*'Harry recognised the debt he owed
Bernard for his introduction to pottery. It
was invaluable in learning to recognise
the aesthetic qualities of a good pot.'*
May Davis

**Harry and May Davis at Crowan Mill Pottery,
Cornwall.**

Harry Davis applied for the pottery class at art school but the classes were full. Undeterred he taught himself to pot after hours. It was discovered at the end-of-term firing that the largest pots, and the greatest number, were those made by Harry. The principal was impressed and managed to get him a job in a local commercial pottery where he was taught to throw.

When the Elmhirsts asked Bernard Leach to set up a pottery at Dartington, he advertised for a thrower and Harry applied and got the job. However, this first attempt to establish a Dartington pottery fell through and Bernard invited Harry to work with David at St Ives. At around the same time a young paying student, May Scott, arrived from spending a few months at a pottery in Malvern run by Muriel Bell, who had herself previously worked with Bernard. Harry taught May to throw. They married and in 1937 set up a pottery in South Kensington, London. During the war May worked with Michael Cardew at the Wenford Bridge Pottery in Cornwall, and also with Harry in Africa when he was teaching pottery at Achimota

Crowan Pottery part coffee set with lidded jugs, glazed light grey and resist decorated.

College on the Gold Coast.

After the war they converted Crowan Mill in Cornwall to a pottery, where they brought up a family and lived until 1962, after which they travelled to New Zealand and developed Crewenna Pottery where they continued their main form of decoration of brush work or wax resist, but increasingly Harry used incision, which was done on the freshly thrown pot. It was covered with fine horizontal lines and the pattern superimposed with broad strokes, using a piece of wood. Their pots were never signed but carried the workshop stamp, a

C embracing a P.

In 1972 Harry and May started a rural pottery in Izcuchaco in the Peruvian Andes, to relieve poverty and help people achieve independence. This proved a testing ground for their ideas on producing pottery from basic local raw materials and making the machinery to process it. Harry made use of this experience on his return to New Zealand and wrote a book on making hand-made machines. Harry's advice was that 'pottery is a valid and viable art-form in its own right, and potters should have the courage to be potters.'

Chantal Dunoyer

Born: Autun Saone et Loize,
Burgundy, France 1945
Studied: Beaux-Arts, Beaune,
Cote d'Or
Leach Pottery: 1967-1968
Lives/works in La Chapell-sous-
Uchon, France

*'The experience at the Leach Pottery
gave me the opportunity to be
influenced by Bernard, who came in
every afternoon and by Bill Marshall,
who was always there.'*

Chantal Dunoyer at workshop, Toulongeon,
France.

Chantal Dunoyer was determined to study at the Leach Pottery, when she heard about the two-year course from her college tutor. The reply to her application explained that they were booked up for the next ten years. She then studied with several potters, and at a firing with Anne Kjaersgaard, met the South African potter, Hyme Rabbinowitch, who put in a good word for her with Michael Cardew.

Michael had just returned from Nigeria and was writing *A Pioneer Potter*. During the period at Wenford Bridge with Cardew in Cornwall,

Henry Hammond, who was teaching at Farnham Art School, Surrey, brought his students on a course. This included a visit to St Ives and Chantal joined them. A month later Janet Leach invited her to join the pottery to replace Susan Smith, who was returning to Australia. 'The experience of working at the Leach Pottery gave me the opportunity to be on the wheel eight hours or more a day, and to be surrounded by a warm and friendly group, while my failure to speak and understand English amused my colleagues and limited my appreciation of their

Casserole.

philosophical discussions.'

The period at St Ives is among her warmest memories. 'It was during the sixties, the flower power years. I was 22 and St Ives was a paradise of sand and palm trees, where everyone met the artists and the fishermen, the land and the sea. I had set off on a world tour to learn pottery, but as it turned out – I came back with a baby.'

In 1969 Chantal started a workshop at Toulongeon, in Burgundy, which is still her home. She throws simple, well rounded, robust shapes. She uses naked clay, stone from Laborne and China clay, 'which reveal themselves as beautiful when the ashes and salt leave deposits.' The pots are wood-fired using chestnut and hornbeam – very few glazes, some slipware. Her three sons and friends help to fire the kiln.

She prepares the clay, cuts and splits the wood and has also rebuilt the house and workshops, all of which she loves doing, but swears she will one day save her energy for the wheel and the kiln. 'One makes pots and one is,' seems to be her philosophy.

Derek Emms

Born: Accrington, Lancs 1929
Studied: Accrington & Burnley
Schools of Art and Leeds College
Leach Pottery: 1954-1962
Lives/works in Stone,
Staffordshire, UK

*'I'm sure in my own mind that Bernard
was not telling people the only way to
make pots was like him. He was more
concerned with quality, sincerity and a
love and feeling for the craft.'*

Derek Emms, at pottery at Stone, Staffordshire
in 1994.

Derek Emms, inspired by Bernard Leach's *A Potter's Book*, studied ceramics at art college and also became a qualified teacher but, after completing his National Service in the Royal Air Force, he applied for a job at the Leach Pottery. He worked there under David and Bernard Leach for a very intensive year.

'I still remember vividly my first view of St Ives and Porthminster Beach as the train drew into the station. I came overnight and was met by David Leach at the station. This was 1954 when Bernard was away in America and David was between terms at Loughborough College.' The pottery was led by Michael Leach, with Bill Marshall as foreman, but both Bernard and David returned. The pottery team included Kenneth Quick, Scott Marshall, Dinah Dunn, Horatio Dunn, Richard Batterham, Peter Wood, Joe Benney, and overseas students from Canada, New Zealand and Australia.

In 1955 he became a full-time lecturer at North Staffs Polytechnic but continued his connection by working at the Leach Pottery through

Plant pot with gold and green decoration, 15 cm high and lidded ginger jar with blue decoration, 17 cm high.

summer vacations from 1955 to 1962. He has exhibited his work both at home and abroad throughout his life. He retired from teaching in 1985 and developed a studio pottery at Stone, in Staffordshire, producing a range of domestic ware and individual pieces in stoneware and porcelain. 'It was at St Ives that I learnt about firing in a reducing atmosphere and this I still do.'

All Derek's work is thrown and turned on the wheel using a light coloured stoneware body and a translucent porcelain body. The main skill he developed at the Leach Pottery was throwing, because of the repetitive nature of producing domestic ware, 'but there were so many and varied stimuli that everything must have contributed to my own development.' His decorative techniques include engraving in the leather hard clay, and brush decoration on the biscuit under transparent and translucent glazes. Reflecting his life in the countryside, and study of textile design, many of his patterns evolve from flowers, plants and trees.

97

EP

Charlotte Epton

Born: Lincoln 1902-1970
Studied: Royal College of Art
Leach Pottery: 1927-1930
Lived/worked in Essex, UK

'The experience of working at the Leach Pottery meant a great deal to her.'
Richard Bawden

Charlotte Epton at Winchcombe Pottery, Gloucester in 1930s.

Charlotte Epton attended the Royal College of Art, where she met her future husband, Edward Bawden, along with the painters Ben and Winifred Nicholson and sculptor, Henry Moore. She was studying painting and design whilst Edward was studying illustration and graphic design.

At St Ives Bernard encouraged her to produce work of her own design in the evenings. A disastrous fire at the Leach Pottery destroyed much of her work and Charlotte left soon after. On leaving Leach she went to Cheltenham Ladies College to teach art. Michael Cardew was nearby at the Winchcombe Pottery. They had both been students of Bernard Leach's and a friendship developed which enabled Charlotte to renew her attachment to the art of pottery. Over a period she collected many of Michael's pots.

Her continued interest in pottery was furthered through working for Muriel Rose at The Little Gallery off Sloane Square in London. Muriel's shop was one of the first of its kind to sell hand-crafted pottery and remained open until the outbreak of war in 1939. Charlotte and Muriel had

Lidded stoneware box, St Ives c.1930 and stoneware vase made with Joanna Constantinidis at Chelmsford 1960.

numerous discussions and arguments on the qualities of hand-thrown pottery. Muriel Rose's book *Artist Potters in England* was published by Faber in 1970.

When Charlotte married Edward Bawden in 1932 they moved to Essex, where her two children were born. The war intervened, Edward became an official war artist and Charlotte moved to Cheltenham for the safety of the children, and taught as a senior art mistress at Pates Grammar School. After the war the family moved back to Essex where she was involved as an examiner in several art colleges.

She was a member of Essex Education Committee, a magistrate and governor of several schools and also ran courses at Denman College.

She began potting again with Joanna Constantinidis. Charlotte had a great 'feel' for pottery, its quality and style, and she has been described as a 'potter of subtlety and sensitivity'. The Victoria and Albert Museum purchased three of her pots. She believed in the philosophy of honesty and good design in hand-made pottery but also appreciated the English tradition of Wedgwood and commercial pottery.

Gutte Eriksen

Born: Rodby in Lolland,
Copenhagen, Denmark 1918
Studied: Kunsthandvaerkeskolen,
Copenhagen
Leach Pottery: 1948
Lives/works in Karlsminde, Denmark

'It is through Eriksen, who spent a short time with Bernard Leach in St Ives in the late forties, that Leach's voice has been heard most strongly in Denmark.'
David Whiting

Gutte Eriksen at Karlsminde studio, Denmark.

Gutte Eriksen set up her first studio with two other artists in Hareskov two years after completing her studies in Copenhagen. In 1942 she moved to her own studio in Kastrup and since 1953 she has worked in her present studio at Karlsminde. In 1948 she travelled to Cornwall and spent two months working with Bernard Leach at the St Ives Pottery.

Later the same year, extending her experience still further, she worked in France with Pierre Lyon and Vassil Ivanoff. She taught at the Jutland Academy of Fine Arts, Aarhus, from 1968 to 1971, 1973/74 and 1976 to 1978. During these times she visited Japan to work with potters and study their methods and techniques. 'All this appears to have added up to a kind of world-view, in pots of great integrity. She has a deep respect for the materials she uses and gives them all the freedom she can. The pots fit into that Ruskinian definition of enriching art.' [26]

However, her pots are not marked by any particular tradition and are not derivative of the Leach mode but, as David Whiting wrote of her recent

Red stoneware pot. 25cm high 1994.

exhibition at Galerie Besson in London, 'there is an understanding of the complexities and ambiguities of form – the object is not only about texture and colour, but also about assured drawing, and spatial relationships.' Her pots vary in shape and size, very large and bold forms, dishes of different shapes, tall bottles, and a variety of poured and dipped glazes which, through repeated firings, become part of the body of the pot, rather than a form of decoration. Each wheel-thrown form is a new pot, an intuitive, yet mastered art of the potter in a creative performance with clay.

In 1972 Gutte Eriksen won the Gold Medal in Faenza and in 1985 was awarded the Thorvald Bindesboll Medal of the Danish Academy of Fine Arts. She has exhibited widely and her work is in various collections in Scandinavia, the National Museum of Modern Art, Kyoto, Japan, Pennsylvania State University Museum of Art in America, the Royal Scottish Museum, Edinburgh, and in the Victoria and Albert Museum, London.

RFP

Robert Fishman

Born: Providence, Rhode Island,
USA 1951
Studied: Rhode Island
College, Ceramics
Leach Pottery: 1976-1978
Lives/works in Rhode Island, USA

*'The lessons, information and skills I was
taught and allowed to hone while at
the Leach Pottery are priceless.'*

Robert Fishman at Rhode Island, USA.

Robert Fishman made his first trip to Europe after graduating from college. It had long been his goal to visit the Leach Pottery and he was impressed with what he saw. A few months after he returned to America Janet telephoned to offer a two-year apprenticeship. 'Being able to work in an environment with Bill Marshall, John Bedding and Trevor Corser and others, especially with the guidance of Janet, and visiting Bernard on a weekly basis and have him handle my pottery was inspiring.' At the time Bernard was writing his final book *Beyond East and West* and Robert was able to read it back to him after his secretary had typed it.

Back in America Robert met Harry and Elizabeth Spring who were running a successful pottery and he took a job throwing for them. He identified and developed a line of suitable functional ware and in 1980 set up a studio where Harry helped build his first kiln. Soon he was employing seven people but fearing he was becoming more manager

Lidded pots, red and green hand-painted decoration.

than potter, he built another, smaller pottery in Rhode Island with the help of one man, who worked with him for 15 years.

Robert developed distinctive and decorative, hand-painted brush work on his pots. He tries to identify and keep in touch with trends in the areas where he sells his pots. The present colours are red and green. 'I believe that's what sells my pottery. The decoration and the colours I choose. I don't think I am compromising in any way. Janet used to say, "Make sure the tail doesn't wag the dog." I always try to keep this in the back of my mind.'

All Robert's pots are thrown on the wheel. He fires in an electric kiln in an oxidising atmosphere where he has control over the colours. He does not make one-off pieces. His goal is to achieve a body of work that will take a lifetime to fulfil and to make good functional pots that people can live with and enjoy. 'It takes a lot of hours to become a potter but you can't count the hours.'

Bernard Forrester

Born: Stoke-on-Trent 1908-1990
Studied: Apprenticeship with
Minton Pottery
Leach Pottery: 1932-1934
Lived/worked in Broadhempston,
Devon, UK

'In 1932 Leach came to Dartington to establish the pottery at Shinners Bridge, and Forrester came with him to build the kiln.' David Winkley

Bernard Forrester at Bramblemoor Pottery, Devon.

Bernard Forrester had already gained his skills as a modeller through his eight-year apprenticeship with the Minton Pottery, Stoke-on-Trent, and realised that production throwing held no interest for him. He had been persuaded to join the Leach Pottery by the writer and critic Herbert Read when he was a painting student at Newcastle-under-Lyme, but even the small pottery at St Ives reminded him of his industrial experience. He determined to make each pot a one-off. Read also introduced him to the ceramic collection at the Victoria and Albert Museum, where he realised the endless possibilities of producing individual pieces.

In 1934 Forrester left the Leach Pottery to take over from David Leach at the new Dartington Pottery at Shinners Bridge, Devon. He also ran a pottery course for adults locally, where he built the kiln and equipped the workshop. Combined with his teaching he made earthenware and stoneware, developing his style. He worked at Dartington Pottery for nearly fifty years, enjoying a long association with potter Marianne de Trey. At his funeral she said, 'there was something beyond the moral and social values that he had and

Stoneware vase 'Swooping Bird'. 12.7cm high 1986.

beyond kindness and compassion which made him the remarkable man we all honour today.'

David Winkley, a member of the Devon Guild of Craftsmen, said of Bernard Forrester, 'It was he, who, with great generosity, encouraged me to start my first workshop, helped build my first kiln.' He had come to Dartington to teach drawing and history, but watching Bernard Forrester throw changed the course of his life. Forrester was also a founder member of the Devon Guild.

In 1952 he started a workshop, Bramblemoor at Broadhempston in Devon, and worked with lustre-fired porcelain in his final 25 years of potting. He was influenced by the jewel-like decorated pots of Persia and the brilliant colours and delicacy of gold tracery in the design. A retrospective exhibition was held at Dartington to celebrate his 80th birthday. Over a thousand people visited the exhibition to enjoy the work of someone who had brought so many students to an appreciation of pottery. His philosophy encouraged learning: 'There is so much to learn, experience and enjoy.'

Kenji Funaki

Born: Fujina, Shimane
Prefecture, Japan, 1927
Studied: School of Education,
Shimane University, Japan
Leach Pottery: 1967 & 1975
Lives/works in Shimane
Prefecture, Japan

'Kenji is one of the most promising young craftsmen, already saying something fresh in a medium of lead glazed slipware.' [27] Bernard Leach

Kenji Funaki at Fujina kilns, Lake Shinji, Japan.

Kenji Funaki continues the traditions of the Fujina kiln which was founded by the Funaki family in 1764. The workshops are on the shore of Lake Shinji, near the old castle town of Matsue, Japan. Like his father, he admires English slipware and this has influenced much of his work, although he has also continued the traditions imported from Korea in earlier times. He left university to train as a potter. He studied with Hamada in 1950 and three years later was invited to produce pottery at Okinawa, where Hamada had worked, producing pots with unique red decoration.

His father, Michitada, was a friend of Bernard Leach, who had known three generations of the Funaki family. Bernard visited the Fujina kilns at Matsue in 1934 and was there to demonstrate and help with the techniques of lead-glazed English slipware, already introduced by Hamada on his return to Japan. Slip techniques were not used in traditional Japanese potteries. Leach also taught the Funakis the art of applying a handle. 'Technically, the way he made the handles of pitchers served as a good reference.'

Stoneware jug, with transparent glassy glaze 1988.

Given these close connections, it is not surprising that 'following the recommendation of Mr Bernard Leach I came to England to study pottery. I mainly trained with his eldest son David Leach in Devon.' During his 1975 stay he studied medieval pitchers, slipware, and the variety of ceramics in the museums. European traditions had a big impact on the Fujina kilns. In a subsequent visit to Matsue, Leach was impressed with the work of Kenji as a craftsman who was using lead-glazed slipware in Japan.

In 1986 Kenji Funaki exhibited in the Liberty 'Mingei' Exhibition in London with Tatsuzo Shimaoka and Shinsaku Hamada. Kenji's pieces were in reddish brown, a traditional colour of the Funaki kilns, with a glaze glassy and transparent, showing the slip decoration beneath, trailed and combed. He also showed Korean-style vases and jugs, plates and boldly designed dishes and tiles, decorated with paintings of fish, hens and other animals. 'I enjoy making my pots and designing my own creations. I use the seal which was designed and made by Bernard Leach.'

Mary Gibson-Horrocks

Born: Kingston-on-Thames,
Surrey 1923
Studied: Wimbledon School of Art
Leach Pottery: 1944-1947
Works in Buckfast Abbey, Devon, UK

*'Bernard Leach was very kind and
patient with me because of my total
deafness, nevertheless he was a firm
and strict teacher.'*

Mary Gibson-Horrocks packing kiln at Leach
Pottery, St Ives in 1946.

Mary Gibson-Horrocks was sent to Bulmer Brickworks, Sudbury, Suffolk to start a pottery for the owner by her former teacher at Wimbledon, Robert W Baker. This was later taken over by Sam Haile. She had a burning ambition to work for Bernard Leach, but at that time Leach did not encourage students straight from art school. Baker then arranged for her to go to Lake's Pottery at Truro to gain more workshop experience.

After three months at Lake's she made an appointment to see Bernard and spent all day at St Ives having an interview and lunch. She then walked to Eagle's Nest for tea, then

home of Will Arnold-Forster, landscape painter, and now of the artist Patrick Heron, whom she later met several times when he visited the Pottery. Other visitors she remembers were Barbara Hepworth, Ben Nicholson and Sven Berlin, who was writing his book on the naive painter, Alfred Wallis. 'Lucie Rie would come down for weekends when she was making her buttons. I sat next to her.'

Mary had achieved her aim to work at the St Ives Pottery. She was engaged in throwing and glazing and was trained by Margaret Leach to pack the three-chambered climbing kiln. Margaret had served for three

Decorated tureen.

years and was leaving to set up the Barn Pottery at Brockweir, Gloucestershire. Mary helped to fire the first kiln at her new workshop.

In 1947 a businessman called on Bernard looking for craftsmen to help him start a pottery in Surrey. She and Michael Cardew joined, followed by two African potters and Margaret Rey, a pupil of Staite Murray and Sam Haile. The venture was not successful. Michael Cardew returned to his pottery at Wenford Bridge, Cornwall, and Mary and Margaret Rey set up a workshop in the grounds of a girls' school; as well as teaching pottery they also made items for their shop in Oxford. In 1949 Mary joined Michael at Wenford Bridge. 'He was a good teacher and helped me tremendously.'

For a couple of years Mary worked with Alfred Ehlus at his pottery in Bovey Tracey which was bought by David Leach in 1955. After Alfred's death she moved to Buckfast Abbey and made tableware for the Abbey shop, as well as teaching the monks. She married in 1969 and became Boys-Adams. Buckfast Abbey continues to be her workshop, 'because it is so peaceful.'

Atsuya Hamada

Born: Mashiko, Japan 1931-1986
Studied: Mooka High School
Leach Pottery: 1957-1958
Lived/worked in Mashiko, Japan

'He faithfully used the method he learned at the Leach Pottery on how to make handles.'

Atsuya Hamada at Mashiko Pottery, Japan.

Atsuya Hamada was very much influenced in style and policy by Bernard and David Leach. He was the third son of Shoji Hamada and also trained with him. In 1972 he had his first solo exhibition at Mitsukoshi Nipponbashi department store in Tokyo, and every year after that. He died in Mashiko at the early age of 54 years and was at that time trying to steer away from the very strong influences of his training to find his own method and style. He knew Bernard Leach from the visits he made to his father at Mashiko and wanted from an early age to be a potter and to study at the Leach Pottery in St Ives. In 1949, when he was 19, he wrote to Bernard:

'We received your letter at the beginning of December. It was the second one we had from Europe after the war. We received your first letter in December 1947, and we wrote you a letter with our news and some photos, but are afraid it did not arrive.

'... I wonder if you remember Mashiko when I was quite young. I am now nineteen years old, and I go to Mooka High School from which my two brothers graduated. I have been studying English these four years, and it seems to me to get harder and

Octagonal plate with iron painting in sugar cane glaze.

harder. I am still clumsy and cannot write well enough. This letter is the first one written by me in English to a foreigner. I am a first-year pupil of the High School. (Our school system was changed and restarted at the beginning of last April) Can you imagine how our family has grown since then?

'... Now let us tell you about our pottery. At present seven potters are working with my father. Firing of the big kiln was just done yesterday and unloading will be on the fifth of January. Many big houses were built (big studio, big house larger than the former house, big kiln which has eight chambers, another gatehouse, and so on). You will be surprised to see them. I can make many pots (vases, cups, tea-pots, dishes, bowls, and so on). I will become a potter. I wish to go to St Ives some day to learn European techniques, and am anxious to know if you will kindly teach me.' [28]

Atsuya achieved his ambition to work with Bernard, and arrived at the St Ives Pottery in 1957.

Shinsaku Hamada

Born: Tokyo 1929
Studied: Arts and Crafts,
Waseda University
Leach Pottery: 1963
Lives/works in Mashiko, Japan

*'Shinsaku Hamada is 21. He is making
pots and will become a potter.'*
A letter from Atsuya Hamada to
Bernard Leach 1949

**Shinsaku Hamada decorating bowl at Mashiko
Pottery, Japan.**

Shinsaku Hamada was the second son of Shoji Hamada. He was born in Tokyo but moved with his family to Mashiko in 1930. In 1950 he studied arts and crafts and industrial arts and technology at Waseda University. After University he began an apprenticeship with his father at the pottery in Mashiko.

In 1963 Shinsaku visited St Ives with Hamada to renew their friendship with Bernard and Janet Leach. They travelled together for a year in America where Hamada was lectur-

ing and demonstrating and also visited Mexico, Europe and the Middle East. It was a great experience for the young Shinsaku, who acted as assistant to his father.

In 1970 Shinsaku had his first solo exhibition at Mitsukoshi Nihonbashi department store, in Tokyo. In 1976/77 he had solo exhibitions all over Japan and became a member of the National Artists Association (Kokugakai). He was also appointed director of the Mashiko Reference Collection Museum, for which

112

Rectangular vase, wax resist pattern with kaki iron glaze.

Hamada was largely responsible for collecting furniture and artefacts in arts and crafts, many from England.

To widen his experience of ceramics he visited kilns in Korea, China and Taiwan. In 1985 he took part in a three-man exhibition of ceramics at Liberty Department Store in London with Kenji Funaki from Matsue and Tatsuzo Shimaoka, with whom he works at Mashiko. He celebrated forty years as a potter in 1989 and held his twentieth one-man exhibition at Mitsukoshi Store, Nihonbashi, Tokyo.

Seiji Oshima, Director of the Setagaya Art Museum, in writing a foreword for a beautiful book of Shinsaku's works stated that although he was always under Hamada's wing, 'he himself most seriously recognises that distinction between father and son is imperative. So Shinsaku consciously made an effort to resist and oppose likeness to develop originality.'

Tomoo Hamada

Born: Mashiko, Japan 1967
Studied: Graduate and post
graduate art, Tama University
Leach Pottery: 1995
Lives/works in Mashiko, Japan

*'I was told the story of St Ives and
Bernard Leach by my grandmother and
my father almost daily.'*

Tomoo Hamada at Mashiko Pottery in 1995.

Tomoo Hamada studied sculpture at Tama University and completed his post-graduate studies in art there. He was interested in pottery from an early age, and remembers the international atmosphere surrounding his grandfather, Shoji Hamada, even when he was at primary school. St Ives was the most familiar place for him in England and the opportunity to visit in 1995 was the chance of a lifetime. 'I wanted to investigate and reconfirm the relationships between Bernard and Shoji.' At the Leach

Pottery Tomoo was impressed by a potter's wheel designed by Bernard Leach: an improved version of the kick wheel, and known as the 'Modified Leach Pottery Wheel'. He hoped the climbing kiln, sadly no longer used, would be preserved, but was relieved to find the Leach Pottery still functioning, with Janet Leach and Trevor Corser still potting, alongside a collection of Leach pottery.

His father, Shinsaku, had also visited St Ives Pottery and afterwards had accompanied Shoji, acting as his

White glaze vase, copper painted.

assistant, on a lecture tour of America. Kazue, his grandmother, came to St Ives with Hamada in 1966.

After finishing his university studies, Tomoo decided to join his father, at the Mashiko pottery. He works with him, enjoying the family traditions and values, but at the same time exploring and creating works that are entirely Tomoo, and different from Shinsaku, Atsuya and from Shoji – a difficult task when preceded by three master potters of the same family.

'I make pots in tune with the rotation of the kick wheel. The process of work from the start to the completion should be done with spontaneous rhythm. I use natural glazes and fire them in a kiln with pine wood. These processes provide the pots with the atmosphere of nature.' In 1995 he exhibited at Togami Gallery in Yamagata City, before coming to Britain. 'St Ives is a beautiful town with blue skies and sea, bright and peaceful. I hope to develop relationships between St Ives and Mashiko.'

Gwyn Hanssen Pigott

Born: Ballarat, Australia 1935
Studied: University of Melbourne, Australia
Leach Pottery: 1958-1959
Lives/works in Queensland, Australia

'Leach's personal philosophy and charisma was strong, and I was introduced to wares I had seldom touched or examined before: Chinese, Korean and Japanese.'

Gwyn Hanssen Pigott at Kelvin Grove College Pottery, Australia.

Gwyn Hanssen Pigott bicycled down to St Ives from London shortly after arriving in Britain in 1958. She met Bernard at the Leach Pottery and gave him, as a gift from Ivan McMeekin, a blue celadon-glazed porcelain dish which Ivan had made. She had been apprenticed to McMeekin in Australia and was due to work with Michael Cardew, during his leave from Africa, at Wenford Bridge. She worked also for Ray Finch at Winchcombe Pottery. At St Ives her contacts with Janet Leach, John Reeve, Pierre Culot, Michael Henry, Clary Illian and other 'fellow pigrims', were all inspirational.

In 1960 she organised her first workshop with Louis Hanssen in Westbourne Grove, London. They got to know Lucie Rie, a walk away, and through her Hans Coper – 'both pivotal for us.' Gwyn also worked at Alan Caiger-Smith's London workshop, having first met him at Cardew's, along with Henry Hammond, Paul Barron and Helen Pincombe. From 1966 to 1973 she was in France renting a workshop and firing in Anne Kjaersgaard's kiln before establishing a pottery at Achères, near Bourges. On returning

Still life with white bottles. (photography: Michael Holohan)

to Australia in 1973 she set up workshops in Tasmania, Brisbane, and currently at Netherdale, central Queensland, where she works alone.

Her present pots are thrown porcelain, and wood-fired. She makes 'seemingly' simple bottles, beakers, jugs, cups, and bowls and other flared or straight shapes in 'still life' groups, or 'parades'. 'The still life groups have evolved gradually, out of the dual pleasures of using and looking. There are obvious influences from painters, Morandi is one; perhaps Ben Nicholson another and my visits to Brancusi's studio in Paris in my early twenties.' Her groups of pots play on the changes of surface and luminosity as much as on colour, form and line. She is intrigued by the fine line between the monotonous and the lively, the dull and the subtle.

'In almost forty years, historical and personal influences are distilled. There has been China, Asia, Britain and Europe – but the work seems to follow itself. There are constants: the scale is domestic, the matter vitrified, the pots functional. They invite food and liquid, but rarely flowers, and they need to be given time.'

SH

Sylvia Margaret Hardaker

Born: Coventry, 1930
Studied: Coventry School of Art
Leach Pottery: 1966-1968
Lives/works in Penzance,
Cornwall, UK

'Bernard would often invite the students, for the evening, to talk. It was always so interesting to hear his philosophy. I always left with a feeling of happiness.'

Sylvia Hardaker at Kenilworth Pottery.

Sylvia Hardaker first came to an appreciation of pots, as a child, through illustrations in the Bible and she would make shapes from clay in the garden. Most of her fabric designs at art school included pots. Eventually she took evening classes in pottery and, once started, she was destined to be a potter. 'I had a Leach wheel made and converted the garden shed into a workshop.'

Sylvia knew of the Leach Pottery through *A Potter's Book*. An approach to Janet Leach for advice on the best way to become a potter was well timed as one of the potters had just left. She was invited to meet Bernard for tea and to talk pots. Luckily Bernard liked the photographs of her work and her feeling for ceramics. Two weeks later she was a student at the Leach Pottery.

'It was a most rewarding time being part of the crew, seeing Janet Leach making her own very distinctive pots and watching her glaze some huge pieces.' Her experience at the Leach taught her to prepare clay, mix glazes, pack and fire the kiln through to the discipline of making

Stoneware bottle. 30 cm high.

standard ware. 'If pots did not meet requirements they would be thrown back in the clay bin.'

In the evenings and at weekends Sylvia was encouraged to make her own pieces which Bernard would price for sale in the showroom or at the New Craftsman Gallery in St Ives. Towards the end of her training she had her own individual kiln, which took weeks to fill. She then had to pack and fire the kiln herself. 'All the potters would arrive in the evening, Janet would provide a good selection of food and we'd have a party.'

From the proceeds of her sales Sylvia bought her first electric kiln and set up her own workshop, Kenilworth Pottery, near Coventry. It was one of the first craft shops in the area and for twenty years she made pots for domestic use. Her individual work was 'Kenzan'-inspired and she used her own glazes. In 1983 Sylvia returned to Cornwall, and now lives in Penzance where she makes pots for her own pleasure.

Peter Hardy

Born: St Ives, Cornwall 1950
Studied: High Wycombe College
of Art, Ceramics
Leach Pottery: 1971-1973
Lives/works in St Buryan,
Cornwall, UK

*'Bernard's teaching made me aware
of form and the subtleties of detail, and
I still feel his presence while I am
working.'*

Peter Hardy at Pridden Pottery, St Buryan,
Cornwall in 1994.

Peter Hardy was born in St Ives and lived in Downalong, the heart of the artists' colony and the fishing community. He attended school with the children of Patrick Heron, Bill Redgrave, Robin Nance, Barbara Hepworth and Terry Frost.

While still at art school he approached Janet Leach to buy a kick wheel and was offered a holiday job, during which time he mixed clays and glazes and made saggars for the climbing kiln. After completing his ceramics course at High Wycombe he returned to the pottery and took over the wheel previously used by Jeff Oestreich and learnt to throw the standard-ware pots under the expert eye of Bill Marshall. 'Bill was one of the most expressive throwers of his generation.'

He was fortunate to be at the Leach Pottery when Bernard, although 83, was still actively potting. Every afternoon he would come and appraise the pots, pointing out subtleties in form and decoration. Over supper at the flat overlooking Porthmeor beach Bernard would talk about pottery, philosophy, aesthetics and his own life. 'I feel very proud to have been part of the Leach Pottery at

Caddy and cheese dish, hand-painted stoneware.

this time,' says Peter, echoing the sentiments of scores of potters over the years. Janet Leach brought Shigeyoshi Ichino from Japan, the son of the family with whom she had worked in Tamba. Peter learned a wealth of pottery techniques and firing skills from him which he would not otherwise have known about.

Peter started his first pottery in Helston, spent some time in Italy, and finally settled in his present studio, Pridden Pottery near St Buryan, Cornwall. He has a large catenary arch oil-fired kiln and two electric kilns. He still has his Leach kick wheel but prefers to use a more up-to-date electric version. He has established a best-selling range of hand-thrown stoneware, distinguished by its colourful hand-painted decoration, which evokes the beauty of the countryside. He uses glazes which he has developed and mixes to his own recipe. Still very loyal to the Leach ethic, Peter aims to continue making beautiful pottery that people will enjoy using. He lives with his wife and family in the countryside, along with four horses, six cats and a dog.

Nic Harrison

Born: London 1949
Studied: Studio Pottery Course,
Cornwall College
Leach Pottery: 1979-1980
Works in Helston, Cornwall, UK

*'An important time at the Leach
was spent in the pot room with the
collection of Hamada, Cardew,
Hans Coper, Lucy Rie and Bernard
Leach, to give inspiration.'*

Nic Harrison at Trelowarren Pottery, Cornwall in
1995.

Nic Harrison was taught by the part-time lecturer at Cornwall College, Bill Marshall, once the mainstay of the Leach Pottery, and responded to Bill's contagious enthusiasm. During the first year of the four-year course Nic worked at a china clay museum, near St Austell, Cornwall.

Janet Leach was an external assessor for Cornwall College and when he completed the course, Nic was invited to join the pottery at St Ives. Although Janet was away much of the time in Japan with various exhibitions, when she was available at the pottery she proved to be a strict, though kindly, disciplinarian. Nic was the last student taken on at the Leach Pottery in 1979, the year Bernard died.

He worked as part of the team which included Trevor Corser and Jason Wason and was involved in producing a portion of the standard ware: soup bowls with lids, small tankards, plates, sugar bowls and egg cups. He took part in all aspects of working in a studio pottery, from clay preparation, glazing and firing the kilns, selling from the showroom, to

Tenmoku vase, matt brown/black body. 25 cm high 1994.

displaying exhibitions at the Penwith Gallery, St Ives.

Nic stresses the importance of time spent studying the work of past masters. When he moved on from the St Ives Pottery and set up his own gallery/workshop, he carried the influence of the Leach collection of pots with him. He found it almost impossible to work in any other way but the Leach tradition: 'It is a way of life; always finding new ways to extend the experience.'

The Vyvyan family offered work-shop space in the old stable court-yard at Trelowarren where, with wife Jackie who is a weaver, Nic opened a showroom and work studio. For 15 years he has produced pots similar to those at St Ives, using the same glazes and clay recipes. He has extended the standard-ware range to nearly 60 items, selling direct to the public and through local outlets. He has designed his own kiln and as well as keeping up a flow of work for the showroom, he finds time for the pleasurable experience of producing individual pieces. 'The learning never stops.'

Michael Henry

Born: New Westminster, British
Columbia, Canada 1939
Studied: Graphics and Design
Vancouver School of Art, Canada
Leach Pottery: 1963-1965
Lives/works in British Columbia,
Canada

*'The Leach Pottery was a great influence
in my life and I made pots for 15 years
with a passion.'*

**Michael Henry at Slug Pottery, Vancouver,
Canada in 1974.**

Michael Henry, after completing his studies at the Vancouver School of Art, concentrated on landscape painting. After a few years he decided to come to England in 1963. He visited St Ives to see Glen Lewis, a fellow Canadian then working at the Leach Pottery. He joined him for a few months, to earn a little money, working as a clay mixer, became interested in the whole process of making pots and the 'communal work sensibility' and applied to work as an apprentice.

Janet took him on and he served an apprenticeship for just over two years. 'Janet Leach was very kind to me as a growing-up potter.' Also there at this time was Mirek Smisek, a potter from New Zealand. Having gained the necessary skills Michael returned to Vancouver and started his own studio, producing glazed stoneware. Two years later he moved to the country about 30 miles north west of Vancouver and built a pottery, making salt-glazed stoneware for the kitchen and table for the local community. This lasted about seven years, when back problems forced him to give up potting.

Since then he has worked in car-

Stoneware pitcher. 27 cm high 1966.

pentry and house design, and for five years worked in graphics for the Medicine Department at the University of Vancouver. After travelling in Europe he returned to his country place where his old 'Slug Pottery' building has become the Slug Meditation Centre, thereby affirming an abiding interest, from his Leach Pottery days, in the community life. There he cultivates a large sustainable garden for visitors who come to camp out, and engages in his favourite past-time of reading in a serene environment.

An interest in natural materials which was developed at the Leach Pottery, a close intimacy with clay, and the idea of 'back to basics', all attune happily with the simplicity of country living in close harmony with nature.

In 1988 he returned to England, made a trip to Cornwall, visited various friends and Janet Leach at the pottery, and renewed his acquaintance with the small fishing town of St Ives which fostered his love of ceramics.

Shigeyoshi Ichino

Born: Tachikui, Tamba, Japan 1942
Studied: Kansai University
Economy Faculty
Leach Pottery: 1969-1970
Lives/works in Hyogoken, Japan

'I came to learn how to put a handle on pitchers and pots and how to paint on pottery in the Bernard Leach way.'

Shigeyoshi Ichino at the wheel at Pottery Village, Tamba, Japan.

Shigeyoshi Ichino began a tour of Europe with a year of study with Bernard and Janet Leach. He is the eldest son of Japanese potter Tanso Ichino of Tamba. In the early 1950s Janet had been welcomed to the mountain village of Tamba by the Ichino family, where she spent several months perfecting her pots. The invitation for a son of the Ichino family to come to St Ives in 1969 returned the courtesy and kindness shown to her during her stay in Japan. In St Ives Shigeyoshi passed on his knowledge of potting in the Japanese style and exhibited his work at the Penwith Gallery.

In Britain Shigeyoshi relished the multitude of museums and galleries in which to see collections of ceramics and other art treasures. London was a convenient starting point for a European tour and in 1971 he was in Villenaux, France, where he directed the construction of a kiln for Atelier du Cep and renewed his friendship with John Bedding with whom he had studied at the Leach Pottery. They exhibited together in a group exhibition at a local gallery in Villenaux.

In 1973 he held his first one-man exhibition at Kotokan Museum in Tamba and simultaneously exhibited

Vase with lugs, ash glaze fired in climbing kiln 1982.

in a solo show at the Turret Bookshop Gallery, London. On his return to Japan he exhibited frequently in one-man shows in Osaka and Tokyo and most recently in both cities in 1994. For several years the Daimaru Department Store in Kobe has held 'father and son' exhibitions. In 1981 Shigeyoshi exhibited with Janet Leach at the Amalgam Art Gallery, London. After he was appointed lecturer at the National Hyogo University of Education, Japan, a great opportunity to revisit Britain came with the invitation in 1988 to stage a one-man exhibition in Dundee, Scotland, as part of the 'Japan Fair,' sponsored by the City of Dundee.

His work ethic is to blend traditional methods into contemporary pottery using Tamba-Yaki firing techniques, based on Rokkohu of Japan. He especially loves to throw large plates, using traditional skills, and decorating with salt glazes and slip. 'I make pots I can enjoy using in every day life. I never become tired of them.' He continues the seven-hundred year history of pottery making in his village in Tamba.

Clary Illian

Born: Iowa, USA 1940
Studied: University of Iowa, USA
Leach Pottery: 1964-1965
Lives/works in Iowa, USA

'Like Bernard I developed a love of articulating what it is that makes a good pot good. When I teach I simply put into words all the things I learnt about form at the Leach Pottery.`

Clary Illian at stoneware and porcelain pottery, Iowa, USA. (photography: John Deeson)

Clary Illian has the fondest memories of her time at the Leach Pottery and immense gratitude for the wonder of finding herself an apprentice. Exposure to the great pottery of Asia and Europe was an 'eye opener' and helped form her pottery vocabulary. Those pots were more of an influence on her than Bernard's personal work – she thinks that is how he meant it to be – but she cherishes her memories of him and his passion for pots. 'I remember how accessible he was and how easy to ask him to critique my own personally produced ware.'

Although she makes objects for everyday use her notions about the significance of form comes from modernism. Her influences were the sculptors Henry Moore, Jean Arp and Constantin Brancusi as well as the ceramics of Asia and Europe. She built up the anatomy of form in making standard ware, learning to throw pots identical in size and shape as required for the Leach catalogue. 'I am quite annoyed when I, or someone, is accused of *only* being a Leach potter because I believe that a Leach potter is influenced by the

Speckled jug. 28 cm high. (photography: John Kostle)

great pottery of the world.'

She lives and works in a converted Oddfellows Hall. She mixes her clay and glazes from scratch and does high fire-reduction glazed firing, and has recently built a second kiln. She still uses a Leach wheel and credits it with many of the passions in her work – her preoccupation with gesture as it interacts with silhouette.

She works in both stoneware and porcelain, selling a range of domestic ware of quality. 'I do not produce a standard ware but if I have arrived at a shape which I think works well and holds some interest for me I will repeat. Fortunately my customers come right along with me when I do something new.' She identifies herself as a crafts person who produces work of the highest quality. Clary is not a decorator. The involvement with wheel-thrown forms makes her trust that the pots will be of lasting value for the user, in terms of utility and their provocative or meditative content.

Dorothy Kemp

Born: Heaton Moor, Cheshire 1905
Studied: Manchester University,
Honours History
Leach Pottery: 1939-1945
Lives in Felixstowe, Suffolk, UK

*'Bernard helped me to appreciate good
pots. I enjoyed the company of the team
of interesting people and "Cornish
characters."'*

Dorothy Kemp, c. 1960.

Dorothy Kemp was teaching in grammar school when she became interested in pottery as a hobby for school holidays. Dora Billington, who taught ceramics at the Royal College of Art, London, and also held evening classes in technical training at the Central School of Art, advised her to go to the Leach Pottery as a student. Before the war Dorothy spent a few days with Bernard at Dartington, making slipware, and during the war she 'looked and learnt' in St Ives.

She became a life-long friend of Margaret Leach, who worked at the pottery from 1942 to 1945, and when Margaret left to set up The Barn Pottery in the Wye Valley, Dorothy transferred her working holiday visits to Margaret.

Dorothy particularly enjoyed seeing a studio pottery at work and making and firing good pots. She set up a workshop at home and also taught pottery. At this time the craft of ceramics was being introduced into schools and she taught it as part of the 'A' Level art course. Her book, *English Slipware and How to Make It*, was written for secondary school

Stoneware jug, wax resist decoration. 27 cm high.

pupils, instructing them in techniques and standards in pottery. This was published by Faber in 1954 with a preface by Bernard Leach.

During the 1950s the Victoria and Albert Museum bought one of her stoneware jugs, along with Leach, Cardew, Davis, and others they were acquiring at the time, to top up their representative collection of a variety of pots and potters. They already had a range of pieces from the Leach Pottery and its successful students, who had branched out on their own, whether carrying on in the Leach tradition, or diversifying.

'I've not had my hands in clay for thirty years but I am still interested in the developments being made in studio pottery. I think Leach caused a sort of renaissance in this field and his influence was great among his contemporaries. Then followed a reaction against this influence, to be followed by a still later generation of potters making good pots and original work.'

Anne Kjaersgaard

Born: Copenhagen, Denmark
1933-c.1980s
Studied: Arts and Crafts School,
Copenhagen
Leach Pottery: 1956-1958
Lived/worked in France

*'The most important element of her
craft training and the essential of her
job as a potter, in particular, was
working in glazes at the Leach Pottery.'*
Elizabeth Gaymard

Anne Kjaersgaard in France in 1960.

Anne Kjaersgaard regarded herself as a European potter, with roots in Denmark, England and France. She had a know-how of dealing with clay and fire that is from the East, and the feeling of her work was Oriental but impregnated by English tradition. After three years at the Arts and Crafts School in Copenhagen she came to the St Ives Pottery and then to France to study and work from 1958-60 at Saint-Amand en Puisaye; she threw and produced in different workshops, Ateliers Gaulier and Pierre Lyon amongst others.

She rented a workshop and started to make her own pottery in 1960. Her first firing was like a hatching or an opening of promises and Kjaersgaard the potter was born. She thought that however many metaphors the clay goes through, whether carved, sculpted and monumental, or pulled, flattened, stretched, it is simply 'potting'. Her forms were traditional, jugs, plates, bottles, bowls. She did not depart from their utilitarian destination. 'I am a potter,' was how she defined herself.

She experimented and manipulated natural materials over a long period. The glazes were transparent

Decorated lustre vase. 25 cm high.

or deep but always sumptuous. She did not lay down a formula and decorated very quickly, using swift brush strokes in an uninterrupted movement, as if writing. An extremely simplified vocabulary tells of the sea and the waves, the undulations of corn in the wind, the branches of a tree, or a bird.

In 1976 she was invited by the University of Boulder in America, to visit for a term of teaching. During her seven months she built a kiln, to the amazement of the students who were expecting something much less ambitious.

Anne lived near Villeneuve sur Lot in France in 1979. By chance she found a kiln to rent at la Borne. The making of pottery in Europe has always been in the traditional domestic style, of shaping very spontaneously, where all the movements of the hands of the potter remain: the impurities in the clay, marks from turning, finger prints, hand prints that have seized the pot only just finished off the wheel. These things she admired; the way handles were put on and accidents and deformations which occurred in the firing, all added to the decoration.

133

William H Klock

Born: Orwigsburg, Pennsylvania,
USA 1933
Studied: Fine Art, Ceramics,
New York University
Leach Pottery 1975-1976
Lives/works in Morrisonville,
New York, USA

*'During my lifetime there have been few
events more important than my year at
the Leach Pottery. My experiences have
left an indelible imprint on my work in
clay and as a teacher of ceramics.'*

**William Henry Klock at Klockhollow Pottery,
Morrisonville, NY.**

William Klock began his interest in clay in America by way of Bernard Leach's *A Potter's Book*. He had written letters to Leach over several years indicating his interest in studying with him. Finally, his wish was fulfilled by an invitation from Janet to come to St Ives for an interview. At this point he was already an established potter teaching studio pottery at a university in the USA. He arrived with his wife and three young sons and took a house in Hellesvean. 'Rosedale' was of particular importance because it had one of Bernard's ceramic horses attached to the ridge tiles.

One of the great lessons learned by William at the Leach Pottery and emphasised by both Bill Marshall and Bernard Leach in their discussions of pots, was the importance of simplicity and directness of execution within the limitations of the clays, glazes and the kiln: never force an outcome. He has a wood-fired kiln but does not fire often. His workshop routine and studio equipment are similar to that of the Leach Pottery. 'One could say my mentality in clay really developed there.'

Consequently, William has pursued

Stoneware bottle. 30 cm high.

an economy-of-means approach with materials and firing. He works primarily in stoneware, limiting himself to a few slips and glazes to get the most from the least. His work develops in series, permitting him to make visual comparisons and decisions, whereby a progression occurs by which ideas and forms take on subtle meaning and importance.

Bernard's descriptions of Korean ceramics, why he considered them monumental and how they had influenced his theories of form, were so intriguing that in 1989 William went to Korea to live and work with Korean craftsmen. He discovered the Onggi potters, who made utilitarian ware ranging in size from small to very large pots that require considerable strength and concentration. Since his return to the States he has lectured and written articles on Korean Onggi and realised the Korean roots in his own work.

He was recently awarded the title of Professor Emeritus, State University of New York. He and his wife run a studio/showroom in upstate New York, near Plattsburgh.

John Leach

Born: Pottery Cottage, St Ives,
Cornwall 1939
Studied: with David Leach,
Ray Finch, Colin Pearson
Leach Pottery: 1960-1963
Lives/works in Langport,
Somerset, UK

*'Grandfather would talk about pots
in relation to other arts, music or
poetry. He would tell me to look at
a thirteenth-century jug and then I
knew and understood what he had
described in words.'*

John Leach at Mulchelney Pottery showroom in
1995.

John Leach is happy as a third generation potter in the Leach line. He
was taught to make pots that have
integrity, that one feels sincere about.
'Making shapes that I have designed,
that are blessed with fire, that people
buy to give you a living – to be able to
do that is wonderful. I feel privileged
that society has allowed me to live in
this way.'

Before returning to St Ives John
worked with his father David, Ray
Finch, and Colin Pearson. 'It humbled
me to work with grandfather. At the
age of 20 I thought I could show what
throwing was about.' After working
all week making standard ware from
the catalogue the students were
encouraged to produce work of their
own choosing. 'My pots came out of
the kiln and were put beside the
others to await criticism. Grandfather
paused before mine and said, "Too
much up here (pointing to his head),
not enough here (pointing to his
stomach), and your tail is wagging."'

When he left the Leach Pottery in
1963 he helped set up a pottery with
Harold Guilland in California and
taught at summer school. Through
the years he has continued to study
pots from different centuries and

Wood-fired oven-to-tableware.

cultures. He travelled to Nigeria to observe the large-bellied coiled pots made by women potters, and likes the early American stoneware whiskey jugs, as well as admiring the work of many contemporary potters. 'When I drink a cup of coffee I choose a mug made by one of my many potter friends. In that way I can commune with that person.'

John's stoneware is robust, service-able and traditional. He enjoys making bowls, and all turned ware. He uses west country clays. 'I love wood firing. The best pots at St Ives came from the second chamber, which was wood-fired. I love that unpredictable, toasted effect from the fly ash.' The wood burned is from used timber. He has planted trees in several acres he bought from a local farmer and is replacing this renew-able resource, returning to nature that which helped him to create in clay.

Mulchelney Pottery, a thatched cottage in Somerset, is a wonderful working and living environment where he makes pots for eating, drinking and enjoying.

Margaret Leach

Born: Cheshire 1918
Studied: Liverpool School of Art
Leach Pottery: 1941-1945
Lives in Ely, Cambridge, UK

'Bernard's insistence that pots are made to be used and that from using them daily one's perception is increased and refined, continues to be one of my principles.'

Margaret Leach at the Barn Pottery, Gloucestershire in 1948.

Margaret Leach first became acquainted with the Leach Pottery when she spent two months of her summer vacation there while studying ceramics at Liverpool School of Art from 1936 to 1939. In 1941 she joined the pottery team which later included Dick Kendall and Patrick Heron, who had been detailed to the pottery as conscientious objectors. Later they were joined by Aileen Newton. When, after three years, Margaret had to leave because her mother was ill, Valerie Bond (Prescott) took her place.

In 1946 Margaret took over the Barn Pottery in Brockweir, Gloucestershire. Her pottery seal was two Ws overlaid, standing for Wye Valley. She took on two or three students and worked in slipware until 1950 when the tenancy of the Barn ran out. One of the students, Lewis Groves, had started a small workshop about six miles away and she joined in that venture. 'Without the training I received from Bernard Leach, I could never have done all this.' She also remembers that all students at St Ives were gently warned, 'It takes twenty years to make a potter.'

She chose to work in slipware

Pots and plates at Barn Pottery 1948.

entirely and regarded this as her natural medium. Her pots were all red earthenware, with glazes ranging from dark brown/black to russet and golden yellow. Although the experience of firing to stoneware temperatures was useful she had no wish to move on to stoneware.

The Leach teaching gave her an understanding and love of clay which to this day she expresses as though still engaged in the craft, although she hasn't potted for many years. In 1994 she said, 'The love of clay is fortified by digging, weathering and preparing it. The relationship of body and glaze, jug and handle, or use of decoration is a subtlety that must be deeply felt.'

The final move to a community centre, at Upton-St-Leonards, where she worked for six years, completes her story. She married in 1956 and became Mrs Heron (not the painter Heron) and sadly, as with so many women artists, this ended her career as a potter. Several of her pieces are in the collection of the Victoria and Albert Museum.

Michael Leach

Born: Tokyo, Japan 1913-1985
Studied: Cambridge University,
Natural Science
Leach Pottery: 1950-1955
Lived/worked in Hartland, Devon, UK

*'Michael derived a lot from his father.
He seemed to assimilate the ideas of
Bernard and like him always made the
best he could from what was available
in nature.'* Myra Leach

Michael Leach at Yelland Pottery, Devon in 1971.

Michael Leach, second son of Bernard, had an early introduction to his father's pottery, where he came every afternoon as a nine-year old boy and was fortunate to know Shoji Hamada and Matsubayashi, as well as Bernard's first students Michael Cardew and Katharine Pleydell-Bouverie. In 1927 with some help from his father and his science teacher, he was able to establish a small pottery at his school. In 1939 after university, and teaching biology, he decided to pursue ceramics as a vocation.

He met his wife in East Africa during the war. There, he was released from military duties in order to build two potteries, the first in Kenya, the other in Uganda. They produced mugs and useful items for the troops but after the war they returned to England to work in the potteries at Stoke-on-Trent. On hearing that David Leach was vacating his post teaching pottery at Penzance School of Art, Michael stepped into his shoes. He also worked for his father at the Leach Pottery and shared the running of it while Bernard was in Japan and David at Loughborough College.

Stoneware coffee pot, combed/scratched decoration brown over speckled blue/white. 20 cm high.

In 1950 Michael joined David and Bernard at the Leach Pottery, but in 1955 he left to strike out on his own. He moved to North Devon, bought a farmhouse and converted it into the Yelland Pottery, where he and his wife Myra spent 29 years and raised four children. One son, Philip, also became a potter.

In starting his own workshop he followed the Leach tradition of working with local clays and mixing the clay by hand. The Devon clays were ideal material. He used very little mechanical aid having just one electric wheel, the others were kick wheels. His first batch of pots were in earthenware but he changed to stoneware, making domestic articles for the table and decorative individual pieces. His pots were the natural colours of browns, greens and greys and a wood ash for glaze bought from a local farm.

Like his father he trained many potters and always had students. He carried on the ideas of the Leach Pottery in keeping to basics and training his students to observe the fundamentals of nature. In 1995 a memorial exhibition was held at the North Devon Museum in Barnstaple.

Warren MacKenzie
Alix MacKenzie 1922-1962

Born: Kansas City, Missouri
USA, 1924
Studied: Art Institute of Chicago
Leach Pottery: 1949-1952
Lives/works in Minnesota, USA

'Bernard Leach was the most important influence on my life that ever was. I know that his example as a person of conviction and integrity showed me how to live.'

Warren MacKenzie at Stillwater, Minnesota, USA.

Warren MacKenzie and his wife Alix lived for two years in the pottery cottage at St Ives with Bernard Leach and learned much of value from their conversations with him. 'He taught me to see, to think and to feel. Nothing is as important as those things.'

Although Warren and Alix had studied at an American art school they found the training in ceramics inadequate. However, Bernard saw potential in them and after nearly a year they developed competence in throwing and producing standard ware. Anxious to experiment and develop their own ideas they worked weekends and evenings building up a collection of pots and hiring space in the kiln for firing.

In 1952 the MacKenzies returned to America. A year later Warren was appointed lecturer at the University of Minnesota, but continued with his pottery. They acquired a farmhouse with workshop at Stillwater, Minnesota and built a two-chambered climbing kiln. Alix decorated most of the pots. She also threw. She used decoration to bring out the indi-

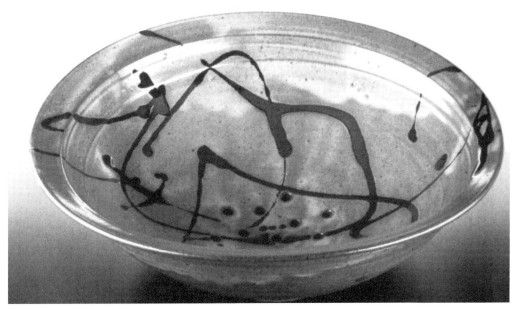

Stoneware colander. 14 cm x 36 cm 1990.

vidual character of the pot. After Alix's death, Warren concentrated on form, surface, texture and colour.

Warren uses an adaptation of the wheel originally built for the St Ives Pottery by Dicon Nance, a local furniture maker. The use of a large kiln and reduction firing encourages the unexpected. He thinks functional pottery is the higher form of art, the 'real point' being that they are designed to be handled. 'My pots are utilitarian pots that people can use in their homes and this is a direct result of my contact with Bernard.' He is convinced that without Bernard's pioneering leadership pottery made by the individual craftsman would not have realised the acclaim it enjoys today.

Every potter decides what his ideals are and for MacKenzie the emphasis is clear: 'I am a potter; a maker of containers and useful objects. The repetition of form and ideas over months and even years allows them to sink into the subconscious and to surface again, transmuted by changes in myself and in my environment.'

ℳ

Scott Marshall

Born: St Ives, Cornwall 1936
Studied: Leach apprentice
Leach Pottery: 1951-1961
Lives/works in St Just, Cornwall, UK

'The experience gained at the Leach Pottery gave me a good all round training and basically I am continuing that knowledge in my own work.'

Scott Marshall at Boscean Pottery, St Just, Cornwall.

Scott Marshall was the last of the apprentice potters to work at the Leach Pottery. As a young man he lived close by and often visited the workshop to watch his uncle, Bill Marshall, at his work. It was a natural progression from leaving school to be taken on as an apprentice.

Although he had no art school background he gained his knowledge from five years' experience in a working environment. He received his training from Bill and Kenneth Quick and from everyone else who was working there, especially David and Michael Leach. 'Bernard was at this time largely creating his own work, but was around to criticise the pots being produced and to ensure the maintenance of quality.'

During his five-year apprenticeship Scott learnt to throw pots to a precise size and weight and to produce a repetition of bowls, mugs, plates and a variety of domestic items, often working from a drawing or photograph. 'I have carried on in the same tradition because I enjoy making pots

A corner of the pottery.

which have a useful purpose.'

In 1961 he started the Boscean Pottery at St Just in Cornwall, in partnership with Richard Jenkins, and created a small workshop, where they took on a few apprentices through the 1960s and 1970s. They built a large oil-fired kiln, similar to the Leach Japanese climbing kiln, which used to hold 1,500 pots. Since the death of his partner Scott has worked on his own.

He still makes a variety of domestic pots in stoneware for the oven, kitchen and table. He uses an electric kiln and obtains 'reasonable results' from wood ash glazes with a combination of other additives to provide variation. He likes having direct contact with the person buying his pottery, especially neighbours and local people, and moves naturally between his workshop and showroom. The pleasure he gains and gives through the making of pots, and the appreciation he receives, is the reward for a lifetime in his chosen way of living.

William Marshall

Born: St Ives, Cornwall 1923
Studied: First apprentice with Leach
Pottery
Leach Pottery: 1938-1977
Lives/works in Lelant, Cornwall, UK

*'Most of the critical training was
delegated to either Bill Marshall or
Kenneth Quick. We learned to see in the
Leach manner which was a very critical
viewing of all parts of the pot.'*
Warren MacKenzie

William Marshall at Leach Pottery in 1954.

William Marshall was born in St Ives. He was the first apprentice to be taken on in 1938 by David Leach. He was 14 years of age and came straight from the local school. He trained and worked with David until 1955 and then with Bernard after David left to establish his own pottery in Devon. He worked at the Leach Pottery for 39 years, with a break during the second world war when he was conscripted into the army in 1942 and returned in 1947. He was Bernard's hands, especially in the latter part of Leach's life, throwing the very large studio pots and leaving Bernard to detail the foot and rim, decorate and complete.

Bill Marshall is a superb thrower. He was foreman, senior craftsman and teacher to many of the students who passed through the Leach Pottery. These students invariably speak of his exemplary skills. As well as creating his own individual pots he had an extraordinary ability to interpret and carry out ideas. Leach would design pots and make drawings and Bill would translate those drawings into forms on the wheel.

Porcelain bottle vase, pale celadon glaze. 30 cm high 1991.

In 1977 he set up his own pottery in the village of Lelant, near St Ives, making his own statements in expressive pots – 'one of the best in the country', so stated Bernard Leach in *Beyond East and West*, published in 1978, a year before he died. Bill worked with Bernard over many years and was influenced by him and the style of Shoji Hamada, whom he also admired.

Together with his son Andrew, also a potter, Bill built a two-chambered wood and oil-fired kiln. As a lover of nature he draws his inspiration from the Cornish landscape, his colours and glazes from the natural effect of lichen on rocks, and the seasonal changes of plant life of the Penwith moors.

He is a reserved, stoic and matter-of-fact Cornishman, and to those who wish to write about him, or even pay tribute, he says, 'You may know that I have always preferred to work quietly and have always turned down such offers.' This does not deter tributes by craftsmen who served under him.

DJM

Donald Mills

Born: Peckham, London 1922
Studied: Central School of Arts
and Crafts
Leach Pottery: Summer 1944
Lives/works in Chichester, Sussex, UK

'I was at the Leach Pottery for the summer of 1944. It was a holiday job, standing in for each person as they had time off.'

Donald Mills kneading clay to remove the bubble, at Itchenor Pottery, Chichester.

Donald Mills was introduced to pottery by Reginald Marlow at Croydon School of Art. He continued as a pottery student under Dora Billington, and stood in for her at the Central and Kingston Schools of Art when she had a stroke. He then stayed on as technical assistant for a year. He met Bernard Leach during the war at the Arts and Crafts Society 19th Exhibition at the National Portrait Gallery in London, where they alternated daily in exhibitions of throwing. He was offered 'bed and board' and a stand-in job at the Leach Pottery, through a busy summer making standard ware. Following this he worked as a thrower at Fulham Pottery, London.

From 1945 to 1952 he was a full time potter, setting up the Donald Mills Pottery, near London Bridge, with Eileen Lewenstein as a working partner from 1946 to 1948. They also employed some assistants. His wife Jacqueline joined him in 1948. She had studied drawing and painting at Willesden School of Art in London and was responsible for the painted decoration on the pots, which were sold to London stores like Heals, Peter Jones, Selfridges, and to America. 'We

Porcelain bowl with grape decoration. 28 cm diameter.

changed our style every two years so as not to soak the market.'

Donald was also involved in designing, producing and supplying a range of pottery equipment, which occupied much of his time for over twenty years, but in 1975 he and his wife returned to making pottery full time at Itchenor, near Chichester. They intended producing Lambeth Delft, but could not find a clean stoneware body ready prepared and, instead, found a porcelain used in making insulators. 'It took some time to learn how to use it because it is not very plastic but it can be worked very thinly. We try to make pots which people like better six months after they have bought them. It brings them back for more.'

He has exhibited widely and is represented by two pieces in the Victoria and Albert Museum collection. The Queen Mother purchased six stoneware mugs from the Arts and Crafts Society 21st Exhibition at the Guildhall, London. Another mark of royal approval was the commission from Queen Elizabeth to make tankards as presents for the coach-men who drove the coach on her wedding day.

J.O

Jeff Oestreich

Born: St Paul, Minnesota, USA 1947
Studied: Art and Art History,
University of Minnesota
Leach Pottery: 1969-1971
Lives/works in Minnesota, USA

'Working at the Leach Pottery had many meanings. It provided a structure to integrate pottery making with life. I am grateful for that opportunity to focus so intensely on potting.'

Jeff Oestreich at studio workshop, Taylors Falls, Minnesota USA.

Jeff Oestreich knew of Bernard Leach through *A Potter's Book*. The ideas and philosophy expressed in that book rang a bell for him and he decided to forward his pottery studies outside the university system. To this end he travelled to St Ives for an interview with Bernard Leach on the recommendation of Warren MacKenzie and, having been accepted, returned the following year to begin his training as an apprentice. 'To be part of a family that was passionate about clay was a gift to me.'

Life and pottery became inseparable. His sole purpose was to learn through the daily making of pots to become a skilled potter. This he achieved, and set up his studio in America upon his return in 1971, working in porcelain and stoneware. 'The practice and philosophy of the Leach Pottery instilled in me a work ethic which has continued throughout my life.'

All Jeff's work is wheel-thrown on an adaptation of a Leach wheel. His original commitment to utility is still important to him, although there are times when ideas override strict function and the pots may challenge the user. He often finds these pots are

Spouted pot, salt-fired. 15 cm high.

successful, and they lead to further investigations with thrown and altered forms. Throughout his potting life he has retained his attachment to a colour palette of Japanese and Chinese glazes. At his workshop at Taylors Falls, Minnesota, he is presently exploring glazes in bands of green, turquoise and grey.

A major catalyst for change has been the exploration of a variety of firing methods, from electric and gas to a salt kiln, but he confesses to a romantic attachment to wood-burning kilns which remind him of St Ives. They require help from friends and therefore fulfil a social function, although the work is exhausting. It also means a search for glazes that will flux in the cooler areas.

His experiences have led him to believe that variety and challenge are elements that keep alive interest in clay. 'The challenge of making work that functions on both a visual and physical level remains a consuming interest.' In 1995 Jeff was artist-in-residence at Unitec, Auckland, New Zealand.

Katharine Pleydell-Bouverie in 1980.

Katharine Pleydell-Bouverie

Born: Berkshire 1895-1985
Studied: Central School of
Arts & Crafts
Leach Pottery: 1924-1925
Lived/worked in Wiltshire, UK

*'It was a great experience and he was
very kind, ungrudgingly generous with
information and suggestions. He did
not know the meaning of the words
"trade secret".'*

Katharine Pleydell-Bouverie was influenced by the Omega Workshops pots of Roger Fry. After meeting Bernard Leach in London she joined him in St Ives, where she learned her craft in the company of Hamada and Matsubayashi. She saw their experiments with celadons, tenmoku, ash - glazed stoneware, and combed and trailed slipware pieces. Her year with Leach proved a turning point in her life. 'I have never known anyone who would give his time and attention so completely to another's problems.'[29] Before he left for Japan Matsubayashi made her a kick wheel.

In 1925 she founded the Cole Pottery at Coleshill, Berkshire, in the grounds of the family estate, where Matsu designed her first kiln. She worked with Ada Mason and Norah Braden on a series of stoneware glaze tests which explored vegetable ash glazes made from plants and trees on her estate. Leach said her contribution had been important mainly in the use of matt-surfaced glazes in the composition of which the Oriental habit of using various wood ashes is normal. In writing *A Potter's Book* Leach asked her advice about ash glazes; he knew of no one who had

152

Bowl with cut sides, cedar ash glaze, grey and brown, matt brushed.
16.5 cm high 1933.

looked into this procedure as thoroughly as she had.

Katharine Pleydell-Bouverie is now recognised as a pioneer in her field, having devoted her long and active life to the study of ash glazes, diligently noting and registering each recipe. Many of her pots were designed to display flowers or plants, and sgraffito or combing were her favourite methods of decoration. Examples of her work, including her glaze recipes, are in the collection of the Holburne Museum, Bath.

In 1946 she bought Kilmington Manor in Wiltshire and set up a workshop in a barn once used as a maltings. Norah Braden worked with her each summer vacation. Katharine used both a Japanese wheel which was spun by hand and a treadle or kick wheel. She used five local clays; one – an ochre – had been in use since Roman times. In a letter to Bernard she wrote, 'I want my pots to make people think of things like pebbles and shells and birds' eggs and the stones over which moss grows.' [30]

Kenneth Quick

Born: St Ives 1931-1963
Studied: Leach apprentice
Leach Pottery: 1945-55 & 1960-63
Lived/worked in St Ives, Cornwall, UK

'A desire to go to Japan and work with Hamada for a time developed, and, with this goal in mind, he saved up enough money for that purpose – we helped him.'[31] Bernard Leach

Kenneth Quick at Tregenna Hill Pottery, St Ives in 1957.

Kenneth Quick was one of the last of the Cornish apprentice potters taken on straight from the local school. He showed himself to be one of the most promising of the younger St Ives potters. He was a production thrower of standard ware but his work soon showed a distinct individuality, which is what Bernard Leach looked for in his students. When he saw a pot on a shelf that he approved of he would say, 'The character of the person who made that pot is coming through.'

When he was fully trained Kenneth taught many of the overseas students to throw. Two potters who worked with him were Alix and Warren MacKenzie who, although trained in an American art school, had yet to learn to make a shape from a specific amount of clay and to exercise critical judgement in the Leach manner. Quick and the MacKenzies liked to experiment and develop their own techniques, hiring and firing the Leach kiln at weekends and working long hours into the evening perfecting their craft.

In 1955 Kenneth opened his own workshop, Tregenna Hill Pottery in St

Two-part egg separator decorated with iron brushwork over cobalt wash, 8 cm high; and cream jug decorated with incised brown vertical fluting, pulled side handle, 8.5 cm high.

Ives, producing items for the kitchen and table, working in stoneware and red earthenware with his own pottery seal and signed KQ. After five years of running a successful one-man venture he took a six months' instruction and teaching post in America.

On his return to Cornwall Kenneth asked Janet and Bernard if he could resume work at the Leach Pottery, to which they readily agreed. He and Bill Marshall were mostly responsible for the training of the new influx of pottery students from art colleges, who were engaged on a two-year work-trainee basis.

After two further years of working at the St Ives Pottery, Bernard and Janet, anxious to encourage the young man in his further development and exploration of pottery, helped him to realise his ambition of going to Japan to study with Hamada. A month before coming home he was tragically drowned in a swimming accident. Bernard and Janet were devastated by the news.

John Reeve

Born: Vancouver, British Columbia,
Canada 1929
Studied: Travelled extensively
Leach Pottery: 1958-1961 & 1966
Lives/works in Canada

*'John was gentle, modest, lovable; there
was a soul behind his searching eyes.'*
Bernard Leach

John Reeve. (photography: David Coleman)

John Reeve was known to Bernard before he came to work at the Leach Pottery. Bernard had flown to Canada in the early 1950s for a series of workshops and was met at Seattle airport by John and his wife Donna. 'We talked and talked for hours, knitting up the ravelled sleeve of time and care. I think it was the next day we parted, almost in tears.' Bernard invited John to work with him at the Leach Pottery. He and Donna arrived in 1958 and while in St Ives Donna gave birth to their first child.

It was Bernard who introduced John to Warren MacKenzie and his wife Alix, the first two American potters who came to work at the Leach Pottery. They became friends and worked together for some months at St Paul, Minneapolis. Both Warren MacKenzie and John Reeve kept in touch with Bernard over many years by talking on tape and circulating the cassettes.

Other companions at the Leach Pottery were Glenn Lewis, a fellow Canadian, Byron Temple, American, Gwyn Hanssen Pigott, Australian, Kenneth Quick, Richard Batterham

Porcelain vase, white glaze. 23 cm high.

and his wife Dinah Dunn, and John Leach, Bernard's grandson. William Marshall was foreman, and Janet Leach had not long married Bernard and taken charge of the pottery. It was quite a mixture of personalities and backgrounds. While in Cornwall John received a grant from the Canadian Council to build a pottery in Hennock, Devon.

In 1966, on the invitation of Janet Leach, who described John as 'a very good potter', he returned to the pottery, but this second visit was not a success. 'I find some things too painful to remember,' says John. And yet the friendship survived. Bernard said of him in his memoirs, *Beyond East and West*, '... his lovable nature and ingenuity always brought forgiveness in its wake.' During this visit to St Ives John was fortunate to meet Shoji Hamada and his wife. He also spent some time teaching pottery at Farnham College of Art.

On his return home John Reeve became a well-known name in Canadian pottery.

Mirek Smisek OBE

Born: Bohemia, Czechoslovakia 1925
Studied: Kyoto University, Japan
Leach Pottery: 1963-1964
Lives/works in Aotearoa,
New Zealand

'Bernard Leach and I met in Japan in 1962 while I was studying ceramics at the Faculty of Industrial Arts in Kyoto. He invited me to come to St Ives.'

Mirek Smisek, with gift for Czechoslovakian President in 1995.

Mirek Smisek came to St Ives to study and work with Bernard Leach in 1963. It was an experience which had the most profound influence on his own work. He was living in New Zealand at the time and the Arts Council of that country helped to finance the trip. He was accompanied by his family. 'It was our great privilege to have Barbara Hepworth as our landlady. She gave me many opportunities to talk with her about art, which has strengthened my belief in creativity and its vital role for humanity.'

He started potting in 1948. His first workshop was established in Nelson, South Island, New Zealand in 1953. Salt-glazed stoneware was his first venture. For the last quarter of a century his studio-workshop has been in North Island, Te Horo, where he works with his wife and partner, Pamella Ann. They make domestic and decorative stoneware and porcelain and have exhibited widely. As well as developing their own work they encourage children from local schools to be creatively involved and gain practical experience.

Fluted branch pot.

Mirek says his aim is to make hand-made things with the qualities of natural materials, to set against the machine-made. He makes domestic pots because he believes an article should be made to live with, not bought and admired on rare occasions. He makes humble shapes, born from the heart and pleasing to the eye, and made as if to use them himself. He compares his approach to the craft with the Japanese tea ceremony. At the centre, the humble pot and everything revolves around it.

'As a potter, my aim is to utilise and highlight the rich textures contained in our clays and rocks. It is important to aim to make a pot which will fulfil our desire and need to surround ourselves with aesthetically healthy objects which should not only be admired for their beauty, but give fulfilment in frequent handling. Pottery, with the exciting challenge of mastery over the elements earth, water and fire, offers tremendous scope for fulfilment. Good results do not come easily, but there is a great adventure for anybody willing to be sincerely involved.'

Tim Stampton

Born: Brighton, 1942
Studied: Canterbury College of Art
Leach Pottery: 1965-1967
Lives/works in County Donegal,
Ireland

'I called into the pottery at St Ives. There I met Bernard and the following day had tea with him. We had a long and pleasant conversation mainly about aesthetics.'

Tim Stampton at the wheel.

Tim Stampton was introduced to Janet Leach through an exhibition at the Craftsmen Potters Association, off Carnaby Street, London. He found his way to St Ives to meet Bernard. At the time he was studying at Canterbury College of Art and was paying his own way through college. He had emigrated to Canada with his family in 1948 and being a Canadian citizen was working as a pottery technician for the college evening class students to make ends meet.

In the spring of 1965 Tim received a letter from Janet Leach inviting him to replace another North American, Jack Worseldine at the pottery. This invitation to work at the St Ives Pottery was a welcome surprise; he had obviously impressed Bernard on his brief visit earlier that year. 'At that time we only had the big climbing kiln, so I trained on this kiln. I built first the little salt kiln then supervised the building of the oil-fired kiln. I learned the value of team work and at that time the different aesthetics of the Oriental approach.'

After two years at the Leach Pottery he returned to Canada and

160

Stoneware storage jar, ash white glaze based on Leach bracken ash, iron handle. 30 cm high.

bought a shop at Indian Point in Nova Scotia, an area which attracted a number of artists, to make a living from hand-made pottery. Some time later he joined the Memorial University in Newfoundland and taught ceramics. During this period he was a representative at the World Crafts Council held in Dublin, Ireland.

In 1971 Tim returned to Britain with his young family and joined the Portsmouth Polytechnic Fine Art Department, where he worked with David Hamilton, who became Head of Ceramics at the Royal College of Art. Dissatisfaction with the art school system prompted him to set up a pottery at Chalk Pits Museum in Amberley, West Sussex. Having achieved this, he established a studio at Graffham, West Sussex, with his partner Ros Harvey. The vast majority of pots produced in the 1970s and 1980s were for exhibition, not functional pottery. In 1990 they moved to Ireland and set up a studio and print workshop in Donegal.

David Stannard

Born: Berkeley, California USA 1925
Studied: Universities of Redlands
and Oregon
Leach Pottery: 1952-1953
Lives/works in Alaska, USA

*'I went to the Leach Pottery because
I'd read* A Potter's Book. *His views of the
unpretentious origins of good work
resonated with my childhood
memories.'*

David Stannard at Leach Pottery, St Ives in 1952.

David Stannard, although born in America, was taken to China at the age of four. 'I grew up in an Iron-Age crafts-economics society. Raised in this tidewater of cultural diversity I returned to the United States with a preference for rural self-sufficiency, where materials which are needed are developed locally rather than imported.' He studied chemistry, biology and the science of soils. With this experience he pursued his interest in the craft of pottery and began work at Tacket Associates, a small pottery in the Los Angeles area that produced quality earthenware. He was responsible for clay and glaze preparation, casting, glazing and firing. Some time later he joined a village of potters at La Otumba in Mexico.

To further his interest David required more experience in an operating pottery. 'I needed a personal place to stand and face society.' After writing to Bernard he was invited to join the team at St Ives. Bernard wrote: 'So much of your beginning is akin to my own that I cannot help feeling that this would probably be the best place for you to come.' After a short time he began throwing

Porcelain bowl. 12 cm diameter.

acceptable pots and spent the year as a thrower producing standard ware. During his time in Cornwall he worked for two months at the Wenford Bridge Pottery with Michael Cardew and the Australian potter Ivan McMeekin, and realised two successful firings.

On returning to America he set up Hill Top Stoneware, Oregon, using local resources, and ran it from 1954 to 1978. Alongside he taught Basic Design and Ceramics at the University of Oregon from 1965 to 1980 and researched the mineral composition of Chinese and Western porcelain stones. His present home and workshop is Local Buoyancy. His quality of life is summed up in a philosophy of 'prospecting, processing, producing, and adding human value to local resources for a sustainable future.' He produces pots which carry the memory of their origins in the nearby countryside.

'I find it almost impossible to tell you anything about my pots – except to caution that you need to put them to use, wave them about, examine them in the sunlight, scrub them at the sink, to form a personal opinion.'

Ian Steel

Born: Saskatchewan, Canada 1937
Studied: Vancouver School of Art,
Design and Pottery
Leach Pottery: 1963-1965
& 1967-1969
Lives/works in Chudleigh, Devon, UK

*'Those four years have affected my
thought process and actions; the way
I see things and do things over the
last 30 years.'*

**Ian Steel salting the kiln, Nanoose Bay,
Vancouver Island, Canada.**

Ian Steel, after leaving the Leach Pottery in 1969, set up a pottery at Nanoose Bay, Canada, where he reintroduced salt glaze, which used to be fairly common, because it doesn't require extra glazing material and is fired in large round kilns used for making pipes. After four years he changed to stoneware pottery.

In 1977 he moved to Devon, making domestic pottery in stoneware, more or less in the Leach tradition. Basically he uses oatmeal, celadons, ash glaze and tenmoku. He likes the quality of the celadons and in the later years has developed more porcelains to use the colours of celadons. 'I like the idea of the contrast between the stoneware and the porcelain. There is a total difference between the two, one very earthy, one very delicate and smooth.'

Ian is not interested in exhibiting his pottery in other venues, or selling through other outlets, but has concentrated on establishing studio, kiln, house and shop together in one unit. He prefers to deal direct with the public. Although he makes functional pots he believes in developing and

Salt glaze pots, tallest 36 cm high.

altering (over a period of about five years) the style of dishes to serve and have meals in. He will often use different clays and glazes. 'Although my pots are for ordinary use, they are not static for me.'

In the mid-1990s, Ian had converted his workshop and barn into a house but hoped to find other suitable premises and begin potting again, and to continue developing a range of porcelain and work with celadons. 'Standards are important and sometimes quite out of line with the usual.' The maintenance of standards was one of the strengths of the Leach Pottery, along with the people working there. In 1963 he remembers the visit of Hamada and Shinsaku and the international team of potters from New Zealand, America, Canada, Japan and the UK.

'In the end I just feel that I have done what I wanted, in the way I wanted, more or less when I wanted, and was very fortunate. It was an exciting time (at the Leach Pottery). Had it not been I would not remember it with such fondness.'

Peter Stichbury

Born: New Zealand 1924
Studied: Auckland Teachers'
Training College
Leach Pottery: 1957
Lives/works in Manurewa, Auckland,
New Zealand

*'Bernard was an inspiration to many
potters in New Zealand. It was an
opportunity to work in a team, to
increase and hone my pottery skills
and become more confident in my
own abilities.'*

Peter Stichbury at his pottery, Manurewa, New
Zealand.

Peter Stichbury, on a fellowship from
the Association of New Zealand Art
Societies, and accompanied by his
wife Diane, spent seven months at
the St Ives Pottery in 1957, followed
by nine months in Nigeria. The experience expanded his horizons considerably. In 1959, back in New Zealand
he developed the pottery at Ardmore
Teachers' College to its full potential,
purchasing ten locally-made Leach-
type wheels and building a kiln.
Visiting lecturers to the courses
included among others Bernard
Leach, Shoji Hamada, Takeichi Kawai,
Michael Cardew and Harry Davis.

In 1963 Peter bought a large old
house in three quarters of an acre
and established a kiln shed and workshop. By the time he resigned his
lectureship at Ardmore College, he
was ready to begin potting full time.
His pots are domestic ware, a range of
casseroles, teapots, coffee sets, oil
bottles and everything that can be
thrown on the wheel. Glazes are traditional tenmoku and a variety of
celadons 'which reflect the lovely soft
hues of our New Zealand environment'. Decoration is through wax

Teapot barium glaze over tenmoku. 16.5 cm high.

resist, iron or cobalt with simple brushwork patterns. Diane is a partner in the workshop making a range of moulded dishes which Peter glazes, decorates and fires.

Peter follows Cardew's philosophy which allows a sense of freedom in the art of throwing and a reinterpretation each time a form is thrown. 'A principle of mine is to make pots to please myself. This is not a conceit, but a necessity if one is to maintain standards and direction, and to develop as a person. In pleasing myself, hopefully I will also please others.' He prefers natural materials and for many years dug and processed a local stoneware clay. He also developed a body clay from four commercial products with additions of feldspar and ochre, which is now successfully used by other potters.

He particularly enjoys making large platters. An iron sand pattern is freely applied while the glaze is still wet, which requires speed and skill. One of these platters was selected as a gift to Queen Elizabeth from the New Zealand Government.

Byron Temple

Born: Centerville, Indiana, USA 1933
Studied: Ball State University,
Brooklyn Museum School, Art
Institute of Chicago
Leach Pottery: 1959-1961
Lives/works in Louisville,
Kentucky, USA

*'Part of my early training in St Ives
involved making things simply and
quickly, and in volume, to get them out
for a price the public could afford.'*

Byron Temple on New Zealand tour in 1995.

Byron Temple doesn't like pots that are derivative. He makes his own with sleek, slim, simple lines and vigorous throwing, with marks left exposed – not trying to cover anything up. 'That's me, my mentality, what I call my ceramic intellect.'

He enjoys creating tableware and is proud to be seen in the tradition of domestic ware potters. He has championed the cause of functional pots throughout his career. As well as making a living he imbues his pots with aesthetic and spiritual value,

although he does not attempt to sell his pots as art.

The strong influence of his years of working with Bernard Leach enabled Byron to produce tableware which is straight-forward, restrained and inviting. He has been described as a 'clay guru' by some of his students, but he prefers to be seen simply as a teacher. When he studied with Leach he went there 'to learn not to worship', or to make heroes.

From 1962 to 1989 he operated his pottery/workshop in Lambertville,

Covered jar, wood-fired stoneware. 13 cm high 1992.

New Jersey, USA. Byron has recently returned from a tour of New Zealand, organised by the New Zealand Society of Potters. His honesty and straight-forwardness endeared him to potters who attended his workshops and demonstrations. From there he travelled to the European Ceramics Work Centre in the Netherlands and was one of only 17 from 120 applicants from 23 countries to be accepted for a residency. He exhibited his work at Museum Boymans-van Beuningen, in Rotterdam, in 1995 and at a mixed show at Galerie Besson, London.

Visitors to an exhibition at the State Museum New Jersey, where he showed 61 examples of stoneware and porcelain domestic ware, were encouraged to handle his work.

Byron now lives and works quietly in Louisville, Kentucky. 'I've danced on the tables, now I want to give my pots more thought.'

JW

Jason Wason

Born: Liverpool 1946
Studied: Ceramics, Africa,
India, Japan
Leach Pottery: 1976-1981
Lives/works in St Just, Cornwall, UK

*'In the workshop you were immediately
into a system where technical problems
had been ironed out and it functioned
well, so the training was really valid.'*

Jason Wason at Higher Botallack Farmhouse
Pottery, Cornwall in 1995.

Jason Wason lives on a Cornish hillside between Geevor and Pendeen tin mines. From his window he can see the weather coming in from the Atlantic twenty minutes before it reaches Higher Botallack farmhouse and pottery. The landscape is rich in the materials he uses for surface texture on his pots. He prefers to explore the texture of the clay, rather than use glazes, emphasising the surface by rubbing iron oxides into the body and giving a feeling of age to the vessel. He collects mineral deposits from former mine workings on the cliffs, then burnishes the pots with a smooth stone. Shells and stones that have been water-washed, rock, bone, crystal, fossil and granite are used for source materials. 'I am searching for a pot that may have a feeling of age but which has a potent presence in the here and now.'

Jason uses a Japanese Shimpo wheel or makes coiled or slabbed constructions. From simple source materials, like straw or gorse from the fields, for firing, he experiments by damping down and laying the pots in the smoke for several hours to

Raku vessel saturated with copper. 50 cm high.

acquire interesting markings. He also uses 'state of the art' technology with an electric kiln of stainless steel.

'For my personal influence I find Janet Leach's work interesting and exciting. Other sources of inspiration come from Korean, Japanese, and medieval English pots and from my travels in Africa, India and the Middle East, in search of a nation's pottery and a concern for its survival.'

He regrets the passing of the apprenticeship system and the limitations of learning pottery at art school. The production of standard ware at the Leach Pottery allowed time for skills to develop. 'Although many students have passed through the Leach there is an immediate recognition of those people, something which is hard to explain, but it has to do with the construction of a pot. It was drummed into you, the way the foot relates to the shoulder, the neck and so on.' His apprenticeship gave him a strong sense of workshop discipline and technical competence but allowed him the freedom to experiment and develop his own designs.

RW

Robin Welch

Born: Nuneaton, Warwickshire 1936
Studied: Penzance School of Art,
Central School of Art, London
Leach Pottery: 1953
Lives/works in Eye, Suffolk, UK

*'I can still see, feel, and smell, the
atmosphere in that workshop to
this day. It was an experience I shall
never forget.'*

Robin Welch at Stradbroke Pottery, Suffolk in
1995.

Robin Welch has worked widely within ceramics but always returns to making one-off pieces. This has been central to his life as a potter. Vase and bowl forms of varying scale and shape have been the constant in his output of individual pots. He experiments with materials on surface decoration, introducing colour with enamels and lustres in mostly abstract designs. His large forms are both thrown and hand-built to bring them to the desired height or shape.

Complementing his pots, and often used as background, are his paintings, which are a reflection of his forms and in their abstraction closely related to the decorative aspect of the pottery. The combination of the two is powerful and evocative.

He first met Michael Leach, then teaching at Penzance School of Art, in 1953. Robin was studying for his Diploma in Art and Design and taking sculpture with Barbara Tribe and design with John Tunnard. Under Michael's tuition he became more interested in ceramics and during weekends and holidays worked at the Leach Pottery, helping fire the climbing kiln and throwing and glazing.

At this time, Bernard had returned from travelling in the USA and Japan

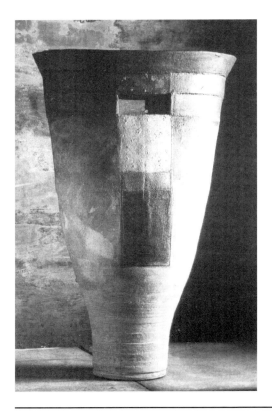

Vase, porcelain slip and salt wash, manganese and copper insets and copper lustre. 80 cm high.

with Hamada and Yanagi after the Dartington Conference of 1952. 'I particularly remember the chats around the fire place in the workshop during tea breaks, with Bernard expounding on some philosophical subject – which was mostly above my head at the time.' His experience at the Leach Pottery, 'influenced many of the ideas and techniques I have used over my 40 years as a potter.'

In 1965, after a period in Australia, he established Stradbroke Pottery in Suffolk. He never forgot the outback landscape which influences his work and accepted the invitation to return to Australia for a year as craftsman-in-residence during 1979-80. Two years later he completed a residency at Indiana University, USA. He is also a visiting lecturer at many colleges of art and a member of the 3D Design Board for the Council for National Academic Awards. Among several commissions he made a large pot for the late Dame Elizabeth Frink.

As well as exhibiting his pots widely he creates ceramic designs for Wedgwood, Midwinter, Rose of England Bone China and Denby.

Geoffrey Whiting

Born: Stocksfield, Northumberland
1919-1988
Studied: Birmingham School
of Architecture
Leach Pottery: 1949
Lived/worked in Canterbury,
Kent, UK

*'Although we have not had much
contact your work is closer to ours than
anybody's.'*[32] Bernard Leach

Geoffrey Whiting at Avoncroft Pottery in 1952.

Geoffrey Whiting was a disciple of Leach. On his return from India as a young man, where he made pots with the 'untouchables', he discovered *A Potter's Book*. It accorded with his interest in Eastern ideas, and gave his life a new purpose. It was also a practical manual and an aid in developing his pottery workshop. He visited Bernard in 1949 and regularly over the next 20 years.

His first pottery was at Stoke Prior, near Bromsgrove. In 1955 he established Avoncroft Pottery at Hampton Lovett, Worcestershire which Bernard Leach visited on several occasions.

Bernard wrote a foreword for the catalogue of his 1960 exhibition in Worcester. Geoffrey was impressed by the idea of several potters working together as a team and created an apprenticeship system like the one he admired at St Ives. He believed in the value of repetitive throwing in developing technical ability, and encouraged a workshop rhythm and discipline. He has been described as a 'pyromantic', one in love with the art of firing and its creative results. He designed a two-chambered kiln based on the Leach climbing kiln and fired with wood and coal.

Faceted bottle, tenmoku glaze. 40 cm high 1980.

His early pots were influenced by Leach but he developed an assured style of his own. He was inspired by English medieval pots and the ceramic traditions of Korea, China and Japan. Individual work was never a priority over standard ware and pots for the table. Bernard thought his teapots the best in England and acquired one for his own collection. He wrote:'I would like to say how very good I think your article was in the last number of *Pottery Quarterly*. Almost everything that had to be said, you said about teapots.'[33] Geoffrey's teapots were chosen for

exhibition at the Design Centre, London.

In 1972 he became potter-in-residence at St Augustine's College, Canterbury, where he combined teaching and pottery making and established a teaching workshop for King's School, Canterbury. In 1976 he shared an exhibition with the painter Duncan Grant at Lewes, Sussex, and was represented in 'The Leach Tradition' at the Craftsmen Potters Association in 1987 and at the Galerie Besson, London.

Jack Walton Worseldine MFA

Born: Osage, Iowa, USA 1937
Studied: Kansas City Art Institute &
School of Design and University of
Minnesota
Leach Pottery: 1963-1965
Lives/works in Sedona, Arizona, USA

*'My experience at the Leach Pottery
and the day to day contact with
Bernard will remain for me an
unforgettable experience.'*

Jack Worseldine outside his pottery in 1985.

Jack Worseldine, before engaging in further study and following a career in the arts, served from 1955 to 1959 in the United States Navy. He came to St Ives after completing his degree in fine art. He was a friend of Warren MacKenzie, who had studied with Leach and who helped secure the position at the pottery in August 1963. During his stay in Cornwall he exhibited in St Ives and in the 'Bernard Leach Potters' Exhibition' of 1964 at the British Crafts Centre, London.

He enjoyed a working relationship with Janet Leach during his two years at St Ives and became a close friend of Bill Marshall, whom he considered a 'great thrower'. He met Shoji Hamada and his son Shinsaku when they visited Janet and Bernard, 'which was a privilege for all of us there at the time'. They had travelled from Japan to attend a major exhibition of Hamada's pots at the Haymarket in London in 1963.

On his return to the States Jack studied at the University of

Group of teapots, white slip, black feldspar and ash over.

Minnesota taking ceramics, graphics and art history and gained his Master's Degree. He taught ceramics, sculpture and life drawing at several schools, colleges, and Arizona State University, while also engaged in producing his own pottery. He exhibited in many mixed and solo shows throughout the United States, winning two awards for sculpture and ceramics.

His approach to pottery has always been functional. He enjoyed making useful vessels for the kitchen, a variety of tableware, domestic items and garden planters. Although he is still surrounded by many of his pots, he was forced to close his last pottery in 1985 because of a back injury and a slipped disc. He now owns and runs an art shop with his wife Mary. Over the period of working with ceramics and teaching, he became a serving member of the American Craftsmen's Council, the Association of University Professors, and the World Crafts Council.

D.Z.

Douglas Zadek in 1995.

Douglas Zadek

Born: London 1913
Studied: Bauhaus, Germany
Leach Pottery: 1936-1938
Lives in Cobham, Surrey, UK

'I liked Bernard's way of diagnosing a shape and analysing a curve. He had a Japanese approach to craft and admired the work of country potters.'

Douglas Zadek returned to Britain in 1934 after the Bauhaus was closed down. He had studied ceramics and served an apprenticeship under Otto Lindig, who was the master potter at Weimar. He had lived with the Lindigs during the time of his studies.

On first arriving in Britain Douglas got a job through Heals, the modern furniture store in Tottenham Court Road. The job was in the potteries at Stoke-on-Trent and he hated it. He then worked for Muriel Bell, at her Malvern pottery. She had spent a brief period with Bernard in 1922 and at different times with David and

Bernard Leach at Dartington, and with Margaret Leach at the Barn Pottery in the Wye Valley.

In London Douglas met Bernard Leach in a gallery in Sloane Square, and liked his slipware pottery. Bernard asked him to come to St Ives. Harry and May Davis were leaving to set up a pottery in South Kensington, and Douglas would be their replacement. He lived in the pottery cottage and struck up a friendship with Dicon Nance, who with his brother Robin ran a furniture workshop in St Ives. They made many of the Leach wheels.

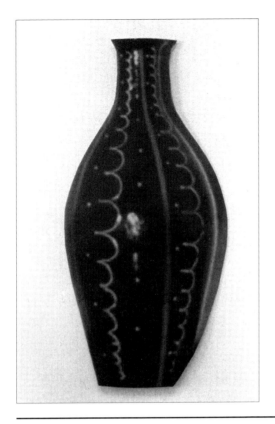
Slipware vase. 40 cm high.

From 1947 to 1956 Douglas ran Surrey Pottery Limited with a partner, making slip colours, which were suddenly very popular and he was able to employ seven people. Instead of using coloured glaze he was using coloured slips as decoration. He then helped start the Craftsmen Potters Association. At the Potters Croft in Oxshott he worked for Denise and Rosemary Wren, who were potting in the William Morris tradition.

Throughout his wide career Douglas retained his interest in 'designing for a purpose', a tradition which involved problem solving and came from his Bauhaus background and training. He was asked to design ash trays for British Airways, using their speed bird motif, and had commissions from Lawleys China and the Royal Mail.

Douglas had kept in contact with the Leach family until Bernard died and had treasured his friendship. 'He was a fascinating and knowledgeable man to talk to. Although our background and philosophies involving pots were so different, it provided a subject for endless discussion.'

THE LEACH POTTERS

Potters profiled	Dates at the Pottery
BERNARD LEACH	1920-1979
SHOJI HAMADA	1920-1923
DAVID LEACH	1930-1955
JANET LEACH	1956 TO PRESENT
RICHARD BATTERHAM	1957-1958
CECIL BAUGH	1948-1950
JOHN BEDDING	1969-1971
	& 1973-1979
VALERIE BOND	1945-1946
IAN BOX	1974-1975
NORAH BRADEN	1925-1927
ALAN BROUGH	1968-1972
TONY BURGESS	1965-1967
MICHAEL CARDEW	1923-1926
MICHAEL CARTWRIGHT	1973-1975
LEN CASTLE	1955-1957
VALENTINOS CHARALAMBOUS	1950-1951
TREVOR CORSER	1966 TO PRESENT
HARRY & MAY DAVIS	1933-1937
CHANTAL DUNOYER	1967-1968
DEREK EMMS	1954-1955
CHARLOTTE EPTON	1927-1930
GUTTE ERIKSEN	1948
ROBERT FISHMAN	1976-1978
BERNARD FORRESTER	1932-1933
KENJI FUNAKI	1977 VISITOR
MARY GIBSON-HORROCKS	1944-1947
ATSUYA HAMADA	1957-1958
SHINSAKU HAMADA	1963
TOMOO HAMADA	1995 VISITOR
GWYN HANSSEN PIGOTT	1958-1959
SYLVIA HARDAKER	1966-1968

PETER HARDY	1971-1973
NIC HARRISON	1979-1980
MICHAEL HENRY	1963-1965
SHIGEYOSHI ICHINO	1969-1971
CLARY ILLIAN	1964-1965
DOROTHY KEMP	1939-1945
ANNE KJAERSGAARD	1956-1958
WILLIAM HENRY KLOCK	1975-1976
JOHN LEACH	1960-1963
MARGARET LEACH	1942-1945
MICHAEL LEACH	1950-1955
WARREN & ALIX MACKENZIE	1949-1952
SCOTT MARSHALL	1951-1961
WILLIAM MARSHALL	1938-1977
DONALD MILLS	1944
JEFF OESTREICH	1969-1971
KATHARINE PLEYDELL-BOUVERIE	1924-1925
KENNETH QUICK	1945-1955
	& 1960-1963
JOHN REEVE	1958-1961
	& 1966
MIREK SMISEK	1963-1964
TIM STAMPTON	1965-1967
DAVID STANNARD	1952-1953
IAN STEEL	1963-1965
	& 1967-1969
PETER STICHBURY	1957
BYRON TEMPLE	1958-1961
	& 1978-1979
JASON WASON	1976-1981
ROBIN WELCH	1953
GEOFFREY WHITING	1949 VISITOR
JACK WORSEI DINE	1963-1965
DOUGLAS ZADEK	1936-1938

THE LEACH POTTERS

Potters with dates at Leach Pottery
but not profiled

Other potters connected with the Leach Pottery,
dates unknown

ANNE MARIE BACKER-MOHR	1948-1950
MURIEL BELL	1930-1931
JOHN BEW	1938
ELEANOR DE SILVA	1957
DINAH DUNN	1953-1958
WALTER GEORGE FIRTH	1948-1953
SYLVIA FOX-STRANGWAYS	1926
GRATTAN FREYER	1945-1946
JUDY GARDNER	1952-1953
MICHAEL GILL	1941
ANNE-MARIE HARRISON	1948
PATRICK HERON (painter)	1944-1945
DICK KENDALL	1944-1946
ROBERT KING	1965-1967
JEFFREY D LARKIN	1976-1978
GLENN LEWIS	1961-1963
TSURONOSUKE MATSUBAYASHI	1922-1924
BARBARA MILLARD	1939
KENNETH MURRAY	1935
AILEEN NEWTON	1945-1946
HELEN PINCOMBE	1936
WAYNE PINDER	1969-1971
BUNTY SMITH	1940
SUSAN SMITH	1966-1967
BRENDA TINKLIN	1978-1980
GEORGE WHITAKER	1938-1939
PETER WOOD	1954-1955
WILLIAM WORRALL	1937

PATRICIA ASHMORE
JOHN CONEY
MARSHA COX
PIERRE CULOT
BERYL DEBNEY
ELIZABETH HEINZ
JORGEN JORGENSEN
SUSAN KRAFT
PAUL LAJOIRE
RUTH LYLE
SUSAN MARSHALL
NIRMALA PATWARDHAN
KIM PERRY
MANSIMRAN SINGH
PETER SNAGG
MICHAEL TRUSCOTT
ZELIA VANDENBERG
SUSAN WOOD
ZADRE

Apologies to any Leach potters not identified
despite the author's extensive researches.

BARNALOFT

My room so warm,
My window large,
At the sea edge.
The dried foam
Blows
Along the sand,
Rolls
Into nothingness.
Waves
Burst upon the rocks
Which stream
Like waterfalls.
Sea birds
Balance in the wind
Then streak across
My window pane.
The seventh wave
Comes rolling in
Right to the wall below.
At Clodgy Point
Under the north-west wind
Atlantic rollers burst
Full forty foot.

Bernard Leach, 1965

This poem by Bernard Leach recreates in words the scene from his window at Barnaloft overlooking Porthmeor Beach, the Island and Clodgy Point.

Bernard Leach's view of the island on Porthmeor Beach.

Bernard at his window in Barnaloft overlooking Porthmeor Beach.

NOTES

1   Bernard Leach, *A Potter's Challenge*, page 21. Souvenir Press 1976

2   Bernard Leach, *Beyond East and West*, page 156. Faber & Faber 1978

3   Warren MacKenzie, letter to the author 1994

4   *St Ives Times* 1920

5   *St Ives Times* 1927

6 & 7   Michael Cardew, *A Pioneer Potter, an autobiography*, pages 26 and 39. Wm Collins 1988

8 & 9   Bernard Leach, *Beyond East and West*, pages 216-217. Faber & Faber 1978

10   Patrick Heron, *The Changing Forms of Art*, page 57. Routledge & Kegan Paul 1955

11   Conversation with author 1994

12   Catalogue of Leach Pottery 1954

13, 14, 15   Valerie Bond (Prescott), letter to the author 1994

16   Bernard Leach, *Hamada, Potter*, page 134. Tokyo and New York 1975

17   Janet Leach, Journal of 1954

18   Janet Leach, 'Fifty One Years of the Leach Pottery', *Ceramic Review*, No. 14 March/April 1972

19   Janet Leach, 'Tribute to Bernard Leach', *Ceramic Review* No.58 July/Aug 1979

20   Karin Fernald, Leach Profile 'What Can a Potter Say?' BBC

21   Oshiko Uchida, newspaper article written in English, Japan 1954

22   Janet Leach 1995

23   Bernard Leach, *Hamada, Potter*, page 134. Tokyo and New York 1975

24   *Ceramic Review* March/April No.122, 1990

25   Michael Cardew, *A Pioneer Potter*, page 11. Wm Collins 1988

26   David Whiting, 'Gutte Eriksen', *Studio Pottery* No. 16 Aug/Sept 1995

27   Bernard Leach, *A Potter in Japan 1952-54*, page 93. Faber & Faber 1960

28   Bernard Leach, *Hamada, Potter*, page 115. Tokyo and New York 1975

29, 30   *Katharine Pleydell-Bouverie, A Potter's Life 1895-1985*, Crafts Council 1986

31   Bernard Leach, *Beyond East and West*, page 259. Faber & Faber 1978

32, 33   Bernard Leach, letter to Geoffrey Whiting November 7th,1955

Glossary of terms

Ashes
The remains of trees, plants, bones used by the potter as a source of body and glaze fluxes.

Biscuit
First firing.

Body
The clay of which a pot is made.

Celadon
A grey-green to grey-blue stoneware and porcelain glaze.

Clay
Basic material refined and processed by the potter.

Earthenware
Pottery made of a porous body which is waterproofed, if necessary, by a covering glaze.

Enamel
A soft-melting glass used to decorate pottery, metal and glass.

English slipware
Lead-glazed pottery, usually on a red body and decorated with slip by dipping, trailing and sgraffito.

Firing
The burning or stoking of a kiln. The process of conversion from clay to pot.

Glaze
A layer of glass which is fused into place on a pottery body.

Porcelain
Applies to pottery which is white, vitri-fied and translucent.

Raku
A Japanese method of firing pots at low temperature.

Sgraffito
Scratched decoration on the body of a pot.

Slip
A mixture of clay and water used for coating clays.

Slipware
Earthenware pottery decorated with coloured slips under a transparent lead glaze.

Stoneware
A hard, strong and vitrified pottery ware.

Tenmoku
A lustrous-black iron stoneware glaze.

Wedging
A process of preparing plastic clay which involves mixing and pressing the clay by hand to expel air.

Bibliography

Barrow, T *Bernard Leach, Essays in Appreciation*, Wellington N Zealand, 1960
'Richard Batterham: Potter', *Ceramic Review* No. 122, 1990
Berlin, Sven 'The Ceramic Horse', *Coat of Many Colours*, 1994
Birks, Tony and Cornelia Wingfield Digby *Bernard Leach, Hamada & Their Circle, from the Wingfield Digby Collection* Phaidon, 1990
Browning, Vivienne *St Ives Summer 1946 The Leach Pottery*, The Book Gallery 1995
Cardew, Michael *Pioneer Pottery*, Longmans, 1969
Cardew, Michael *A Pioneer Potter, An autobiography*. Wm Collins, 1988
Carter, Pat *A Dictionary of British Studio Potters*, Scolar Press, 1990
Clark ,Garth *Michael Cardew, An intimate account of a potter who has captured the spirit of country craft*, Faber & Faber, 1978
Clark, Garth *The Potter's Art*, Phaidon, 1995
Craft Potters Association *10th Edition Illustrated Directory of Fellows & Professional members*, Ceramic Review Publishing, 1994
Crafts Council *Katharine Pleydell-Bouverie: A Potter's Life*, 1986
Dartington Cider Press *Dartington 60 years of Pottery 1933-1993*, 1993
Harry Davis: The Complete Potter, tributes in *Ceramic Review*, No.109, 1988
Davis, May *May, Her Story*, New Zealand, 1990
Fournier, Robert *David Leach, A Potter's Life*, 1977, monograph edited from tapes made by Bernard and David Leach, Lacock, 1977
Fournier, Robert and Sheila *A Guide to Public Collections of Studio Pottery in the British Isles*, Ceramic Review Publishing, 1994
Galerie Besson catalogue *Gutte Eriksen*, 1995
Gaymard, Elisabeth 'Anne Kjaersgaard', *La Revue de la Ceramique et du Verre*, 1985
Hoghen, Carol *The Art of Bernard Leach*, Faber & Faber, 1978
Kemp, Dorothy *English Slipware and How to Make it*, Faber & Faber, 1954

Lane, W H *Bernard Leach: Ceramics* Auction Catalogue, Penzance, 1980
Lane, W H *Leach Bernard, Shoji Hamada* , Auction Catalogue, Penzance, 1981
Lay, David *British Studio Pottery*, Auction Catalogue, Penzance, 1994
Leach, Bernard *A Potter's Outlook*, London, 1928
Leach, Bernard, *A Potter's Book*, Faber, 1940 (and later editions)
Leach, Bernard *The Leach Pottery 1920-1946*, Berkeley Galleries, 1946
Leach, Bernard 'The Contemporary Studio-Potter', *Potters' Quarterly*, 1948
Leach, Bernard *A Potter's Portfolio, A selection of fine pots*, Lund Humphries, 1951
Leach, Bernard '*The Leach Pottery 1920-1952*', 1952
Leach, Bernard Letter to Geoffrey Whiting, November 7th, 1955
Leach, Bernard *A Potter in Japan 1952-54*, Faber & Faber, 1960
Leach, Bernard *Kenzan & his tradition. The Lives & Times of Koetsu, Sotatsu, Korin & Kenzan*, Faber, 1966
Bernard Leach and Barbara Hepworth: A compendium compiled by St Ives Council, Honorary Freedom of the Borough, 1968
Leach, Bernard *Drawings, Verse and Belief*. Jupiter Books, 1973
Leach, Bernard *A Potter's Work*, London, 1967
Leach, Bernard *Hamada, Potter*, Tokyo and New York, 1975
Leach, Bernard *A Potter's Challenge*, Souvenir Press, 1976
Leach, Bernard *Beyond East & West: Memoirs, Portraits & Essays*, Faber, 1978
Leach, Janet 'Going to Pot', *Ceramic Review* No. 71, Sept/Oct 1981
Leach, Janet 'Fifty One Years of the Leach Pottery', *Ceramic Review* No. 14, 1972
Lewis, David *Warren MacKenzie, An American Potter*, Kodansha International, 1991
Moncrieff, Elspeth 'Norah Braden: A talent long lain dormant' (newspaper article unknown source), 1995
Naylor, Barrie *Quakers in the Rhondda*

Rice, Paul and Christopher Gowing *British Studio Ceramics in the 20th Century*, Barrie and Jenkins, London, 1989

Rose, Muriel *Artist Potters in England*, Faber & Faber, 1955, 1970 (revised)

Uchida, Oshiko, Hamada profile in newspaper article written in English, Japan, 1954

Victoria and Albert Museum *The Art of Bernard Leach*, 1977

Watson, Oliver *Studio Pottery*, Phaidon, 1993

Whiting, David 'Geoffrey Whiting 1919-1988', *Studio Pottery* No.7 Feb/Mar, 1994

Whiting, David 'Gutte Eriksen', *Studio Pottery* No.16 Aug/Sept, 1995

Whybrow, Marion *St Ives 1883-1993:Portrait of an Art Colony*, Antique Collectors' Club, 1994

Yanagi, Soetsu *The Unknown Craftsman. A Japanese insight into Beauty*, Tokyo 1972 and 1989

Films and Tapes

A Potter's World, BBC film of St Ives Pottery, 1960

The Art of the Potter, East/West Productions – 50-minute film of the process of pottery making filmed in Mashiko, Japan with Hamada and interview with Bernard Leach

Fernald, Karin *What Can A Potter Say?* BBC N.H.K. Television, film of Bernard Leach, 1974

Ismay, W A *David Leach, A Monograph*. Tapes by Bernard and David Leach, 1977

Leach, David *Pots*, Boston Radio interview with Dick Pleasant, 1990

Leach, David *The Leach Influence*, Bristol Polytechnic, 1989

Television South West *The Stories of Two Great South West Artists: Leach and Hepworth*, video from earlier films, 1995

Acknowledgements

I wish to thank all the potters who provided valuable photographs and information on themselves and others, and especially Janet and David Leach for reading the first chapter and providing photographs; Sayuri Lily Hill of Mosaic Gallery, St Ives, for Japanese translations; Michelle Wright for French translations.

Photo credits

Cecil Baugh, for photograph of 'Rainbow' pot, collection of Senator Oswald Harding QC; Valerie Bond, collection of photographs; *Ceramic Review*, photograph of David Leach pot; Nigel Cheffers Heard, photograph of Bernard Forrester; Stanley Cock, photograph of William Marshall; David Coleman, photograph of John Reeve and pots; Maggie Geraud, High Cross House, Dartington; Bret Guthrie, photograph of Bernard Leach and Shoji Hamada 1920; Tomoo Hamada, permission to use family photographs; Holburne Museum & Crafts Study Centre, photographs of Katharine Pleydell-Bouverie and Norah Braden; Michael Holohan, photograph of Gwyn Hanssen Pigott pots; Peter Kinnear for Janet Leach pots; John Kostle, photographs of Clary Illian and pot; David Lay, auctioneer, for allowing me to take photographs of pots in his possession; Torquil Macleod, photograph of David Leach and Tomoo Hamada at Dartington 1995; Duncan Painter, photograph of Michael Cardew pot; Ron Sloman, photograph of John Leach pots; Leon Suddaby, Sims Gallery St Ives, photographs of Leach teaset and of Bill Marshall pot; Ron Sutherland, colour photograph of Trevor Corser pot; Leif Tuxan, photograph of Gutte Eriksen; Paul Vincent, photograph of Michael Leach pot; and to Cornelia Wingfield Digby, for transparencies of work by Richard Batterham, Bernard Leach and William Marshall.

INDEX

Page numbers in bold refer to illustrations; numbers in italic relate to plate numbers in the colour section.